PagePlus X8
Resource Guide

Contacting Serif

Help with your Product

Com*unityPlus
community.serif.com
Get answers and ask questions in the
Serif community!

Additional Serif information

Serif website
www.serif.com

Main office

Address
The Software Centre, PO Box 2000
Nottingham, NG11 7GW, UK

Phone
(0115) 914 2000

Phone (Registration)
(0800) 376 1989
+44 800 376 1989
800-794-6876 (US, Canada)

Phone (Sales)
(0800) 376 7070
+44 800 376 7070
800-489-6703 (US, Canada)

Customer Service
0845 345 6770
800-489-6720 (US, Canada)

Fax
(0115) 914 2020

Credits

This Resource Guide, and the software described in it, is furnished under an end user License Agreement, which is included with the product. The agreement specifies the permitted and prohibited uses.

Trademarks

Serif is a registered trademark of Serif (Europe) Ltd.

PagePlus is a registered trademark of Serif (Europe) Ltd.

All Serif product names are trademarks of Serif (Europe) Ltd.

Microsoft, Windows, and the Windows logo are registered trademarks of Microsoft Corporation. All other trademarks acknowledged.

Windows Vista and the Windows Vista Start button are trademarks or registered trademarks of Microsoft Corporation in the United States and/or other countries.

Kindle, the AmazonKindle logo, and Whispersync are trademarks of Amazon.com, Inc. or its affiliates.

Nook is a trademark of Barnes & Noble, Inc.

Copyrights

Introduction

Welcome to the PagePlus X8 Resource Guide.

This Resource Guide covers the best techniques for using the fundamental features of PagePlus, from beginner- to advanced-level, and provides creative inspiration for producing your publications.

1: Tutorials

The tutorials will help you work with the tools and content available in PagePlus X8. You'll learn how to use these fundamental tools and professional features to create dynamic and eye-catching publications. In this chapter we'll offer tips on how you can increase your project's efficiency and will also explore a range of publishing options.

2: Creative Showcase

PagePlus X8 provides many professionally designed **Pro Template** and **Theme Layout** publications to help you get started easily. We showcase a few Pro Design Templates and theme layouts in this chapter. Instructions on accessing these templates and theme layouts are also included.

Working with tutorials

Throughout the Resource Guide, you'll be prompted to access resource files from the **Assets** tab within PagePlus (located to the left of your workspace). These files have been provided to get you started or to help focus on a key learning point. Details for accessing these files are provided within the tutorials.

Useful icons

Here is a quick guide to the icons you'll find useful along the way.

 Don't forget to save your work! We'll remind you along the way with these helpful save points.

 These give you an estimate of how long a tutorial will take to complete.

 For guidance, tutorials are graded between 1 (beginner) – 3 (advanced).

 This is a note. Notes provide useful information about the program or a particular technique.

 This is a tip. Our tips provide information that will help you with your projects.

 This is a warning! We don't want to make you panic but when you see this icon, you need to pay attention to the steps as they will be particularly important.

Exploring PagePlus X8

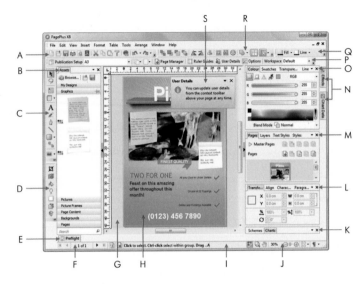

(**A**) Standard toolbar, (**B**) Assets tab, (**C**) Tools toolbar,
(**D**) Attributes toolbar, (**E**) Preflight tab (auto hidden), (**F**) Page
Navigation tools, (**G**) Pasteboard, (**H**) Page area, (**I**) Hintline
toolbar, (**J**) View tools, (**K**) Schemes & Charts tabs (collapsed),
(**L**) Transform, Align, Character & Paragraph tabs, (**M**) Pages,
Layers, Text Styles & Styles tabs, (**N**) Effects & Chart Data tabs (auto
hidden) (**O**) Colour, Swatches, Transparency & Line tabs,
(**P**) Context toolbar, (**Q**) Colours toolbar, (**R**) Arrange toolbar,
(**S**) Smart Hints.

Table of Contents

Tutorials

1

Working with theme layouts

15 min

Theme layouts are great starting points for your publications. They include placeholder text and pictures and can quickly be modified to create a professional publication. We'll walk you through the process of customising a theme layout flyer and show you how to use some of the fundamental tools in PagePlus as we go.

By the end of this tutorial you will be able to:

- Open a theme layout from the Startup Assistant.

- Update and implement User Details.

- Select and edit text on the page.

- Add pictures to publications.

- Explore your publication options—printed or electronic.

Let's begin...

1. From the **File** menu, click **Startup Assistant**.

2. On the left, click **Templates**.

3. On the **Templates** list, select **Flyers** (**A6** sub-category) and, from the thumbnail gallery, click the **Level** template.

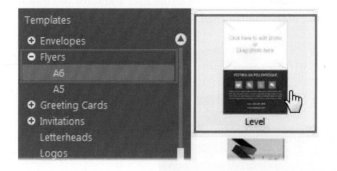

The gallery updates to allow you to choose from three Colour Schemes and two designs.

4. From the **Colour Scheme** drop-down list, select **Level 3**.

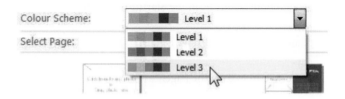

The scheme of the thumbnails will update appropriately.

5. Select the check box for your design preference.

6. Click **OK**.

The publication opens in the workspace and you are presented with the User Details dialog. We'll look at this dialog in more details next.

User Details

The **User Details** dialog provides a convenient area to store information which you might use regularly in your publications, such as your name, company name, address, telephone number, and so on. Rather than type these details into every publication (and risk typos or inconsistencies), you can type them once in this dialog and it will populate throughout your publications.

We'll be focusing on the Default business set which has been presented automatically. However, if you'd like to learn more about User Details and Business Sets, see *Inserting user details* in PagePlus Help (or press the **Help** button in the dialog).

To update user details:

1. In the **User Details** dialog, in the **Name** input box, drag to select the 'Your Name' placeholder and then type your name.

2. Repeat for any (or all) other fields. For this tutorial in particular, **Web Site URL**, **Motto** and **Phone**.

3. Click **Update**.

The user detail fields present in the publication are updated.

We can add further user detail fields to quickly populate the information on the page.

To add user details:

1. Position your cursor at the end of the word 'PELLENTESQUE'. You will see a glowing highlight around the text frame.

2. Click to select the frame text and place an insertion point at the end of the text.

3. Drag to select the placeholder text.

4. From the **Insert** menu, select **Information>User Details**.

5. In the **User Details** dialog, select **(Business) Motto** and click **OK**.

The placeholder text is replaced by the business motto user detail.

Next, we'll look at updating the remaining placeholder text on the page.

 Save now! Click **File>Save As**, type in a new name and click **Save**.

Frame text

Most of the text you use in PagePlus will be primarily contained within text frames. We discuss some of the unique features of frame text in the dedicated *Frame text* tutorial on p. 63, so here we'll just discuss editing text.

To select and edit text:

1. Click anywhere in the paragraph which starts 'Vestibulum velit orci...'.

2. Triple-click anywhere in the paragraph to select all the text.

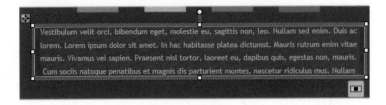

3. Type the information you wish to include on the flyer.

You can modify the text further, once written, by adding local formatting or using text styles (see p. 87).

4. Drag over a word (or sentence) to select it and then, from the context toolbar or **Text Styles** tab, select an attribute to apply.

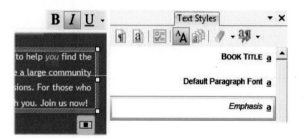

5. If you have less or more text than the placeholder text, you can resize the text frame by dragging the corner and edge handles, and reposition it by dragging the frame's  move button.

Now we've covered the basics of editing text, let's look at pictures.

Pictures

One difference between theme layouts and design templates is their use of pictures. Design templates are populated with royalty-free pictures, while theme layouts have placeholder picture frames which can be filled with your own pictures. You can do this in two ways and we'll show you both.

To add pictures to frames directly:

1. Double-click on the picture frame placeholder.

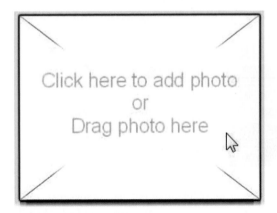

2. In the **Import Picture** dialog, browse to your **Images** folder.

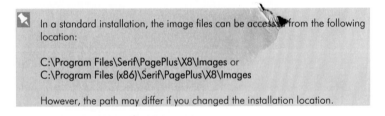

In a standard installation, the image files can be accessed from the following location:

C:\Program Files\Serif\PagePlus\X8\Images or
C:\Program Files (x86)\Serif\PagePlus\X8\Images

However, the path may differ if you changed the installation location.

3. Select **060117a0006.jpg** and click **Open**.

The picture is added to the frame.

All selected picture frames that contain a picture will display a supporting **Picture frame** toolbar under the frame. This offers panning, rotation (90 degrees anti-clockwise), zoom in, zoom out, and replace picture controls.

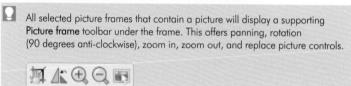

Alternatively, you can store pictures in the Assets tab and then drag them onto picture frames. This is more efficient if you have multiple picture frames in your publication.

To add a pictures via the Assets tab:

1.   On the **Assets** tab:

- Click the **Pictures** header.

- Click **Add**.

2.   In the **Import Picture** dialog, browse to your **Images** folder.

3.   Select one or more pictures (**Shift**- or **Ctrl**-click to select multiple files) and click **Open**.

4. Drag a picture of your choice onto the empty picture frame (or over an existing framed picture).

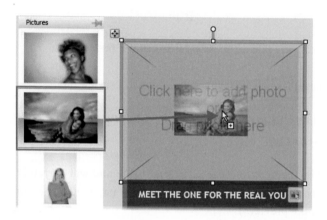

 AutoFlow lets you flow the pictures present in the tab's Pictures category throughout empty picture frames spread throughout your publication (you can't reflow pictures once frames are populated with content).

That's it! Now our theme layout has been populated with our custom user details, text, and pictures, it is ready to be shared. We'll briefly discuss sharing and distribution options next.

Don't forget to save your work!

Publication options

The two ways in which we might publish our flyer is by printing or converting to an industry-standard electronic file. Printing can be direct from PagePlus via a desktop printer or a PDF file can be prepared for professional printing.

We'll look at desktop printing first...

To print using a desktop printer:

1. From the **File** menu, select **Print/PDF Preview**.

    PagePlus will open your publication in **Preview** mode.

2. On the **Printer** toolbar, from the **Select Printer** drop-down list, select a printer.

    The theme layout page size is set to A6 and will currently print in the centre of A4 or Letter size paper. (As you can see in the preview.)

If you'd rather conserve paper and print as many copies as will fit on one page, you can change the layout of the printing.

3. On the **Imposition** toolbar:

- From the **Imposition Mode** drop-down list, select **Step & Repeat**.

- Set **Across** to **2**.

- Set **Down** to **2**.

    This will ensure four copies of the flyer print on each page.

4. On the **Margins** toolbar (at the bottom of Preview mode window):

- Click 🖨 **From Printer**.

    The **Left**, **Top**, **Right**, and **Bottom** margins update to fit your printer.

- Set the **H Gap** to **0.0 cm**.

- Set the **V Gap** to **0.0 cm**.

    This will ensure there are no gaps between the flyers, making them easier to cut out.

Due to printer margins, some of our flyers are cropped and will not print fully.

We can overcome this issue by scaling our printing.

5. On the **Imposition** toolbar, click  **Scale to Fit**.

The preview updates to show how the final print will look.

6. On the **Printer** toolbar, click 🖶 **Print**.

7. In the **Print** dialog:

   • In the **Copies** input box, set the number of **pages** you want to print. For example, setting the Copies to **10** will result in 10 pages each with four copies of the flyer and therefore 40 flyers in total.

   • Click **Print**.

The flyers print (four to a page) ready for cutting out and distributing.

Professional printing

If your budget allows, you can prepare the flyers for a professional printer. This will save you the effort of printing and cutting out flyers as above. For more information, see the *Bleeds and scaling for professional printing* tutorial on p. 35.

As an alternative (or in addition) to a printed flyer, you may wish to publish to an industry-standard electronic file. We'll walk you through this next.

To publish to an industry-standard electronic file:

1. On the **Standard** toolbar, click **Publish as PDF**.

2. In the **Publish PDF** dialog:

   • From the **Profile** drop-down list, select **Default**, **Web - Normal**, or **Web - Compact**.

   • Click **Publish**.

3. In the **Publish to PDF** dialog, type in a **File name** and click **Save**.

Each profile will publish the pictures in the publication at different levels of quality. This will result in the size of the file varying. You may wish to test each profile and select the one you prefer.

That's it! Your PDF is now ready for sharing via email or the web. Why not hone your skills by running through this tutorial again, using the alternative Levels flyer design, or any other theme layout publication?

Creating page layouts

 15 min

Effective publication design depends on a clear visual structure that conveys and complements the main message. The right layout should provide a consistent framework to help you organize page elements, but should also be flexible enough to let you exercise your creativity.

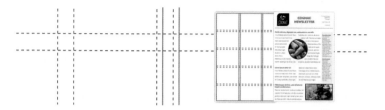

We'll introduce you to the various design aids available in PagePlus and show you how you can use them to structure your page effectively for faultless printed publications.

By the end of this tutorial you will be able to:

- Set up page print margins.

- Set up column and row guides.

- Create an asymmetrical grid using ruler guides.

- Set up page spreads for multi-page publications.

Let's begin...

1. From the **File** menu, click **Startup Assistant**.

2. On the left, click **New Publication**.

3. Click to select **A4** or **Letter** size paper.

   A single, blank page will open in the workspace.

Clean Design mode

In **Clean Design** mode (default), layout guides only display when an object is created or moved near to them. This is useful during the design process but, to help us work through this tutorial, we will switch Clean Design mode off to set up our publication.

To toggle Clean Design view:

- On the **Arrange** toolbar, click ▥ **Clean Design**.

> Still can't see your layout guides? From the **View** menu, ensure that **Guide Lines** and **Bleed Area Guides** are selected from the **Grids and Guides** flyout, and that **Trimmed Mode** is not selected.

Customizing page margins

It could be argued that the most important guides are the page margins, particularly when printing publications on a desktop printer. By designing within the margins you will ensure that all of your design is printed.

To set page print margins:

1. From the **File** menu, select **Publication Setup**.

2. In the **Publication Setup** dialog:

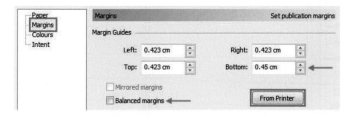

- Select the **Margins** category on the left.

- In the Margin Guides section, click **From Printer**.

  The page margins update based on the settings of the default printer used by your computer.

  You might find, like our printer, the margins are different depending on which side they are on.

- Select **Balanced margins** to ensure the Top and Bottom margins match, and the Left and Right margins match.

- (Optional) Manually update any margin guide value to improve the symmetry of your guides (making sure the values are greater than those generated from the printer).

  We updated our guides to 0.45 cm all around.

- Click **OK**.

Your page margins now indicate the 'safe' zone which you can design within.

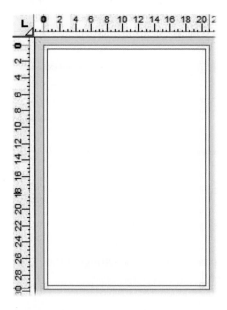

Anything placed within the blue boundary will print, while anything outside the blue boundary may not.

 Save now! Click **File>Save As**, type in a new name and click **Save**.

Setting up layout guides

The grid is a traditional layout tool that provides some crucial functions for both reader and designer. A grid structure, such as the one illustrated below, makes it easier to provide consistency on a page by helping to determine such things as the width of text columns, the space around pictures and graphic objects, and so on. You'll find working with the grid significantly speeds up the layout process.

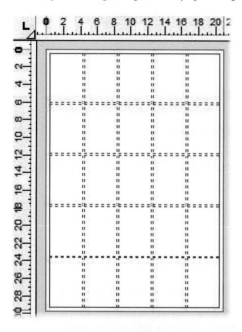

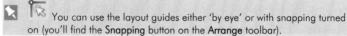

You can use the layout guides either 'by eye' or with snapping turned on (you'll find the **Snapping** button on the **Arrange** toolbar).

To set up layout guides:

1. From the **File** menu, select **Publication Setup**.

2. In the **Publication Setup** dialog:

- Select the **Margins** category on the left.

- Set the number of **Rows** to 5.

- Set the number of **Columns** to 5.

- Set the **Row gap** and **Column gap** (the space between your rows/columns, respectively).

  We set ours to half the size of our margins, i.e. 0.225 cm.

- Click **OK**.

You should now see a 5 x 5 blue grid superimposed on your page. You can add content to your page, using the grid as a guide to line up objects. Alternatively, you can use the grid as a temporary intermediate step for setting up other guides (see *Creating an asymmetrical grid using ruler guides* on p. 26).

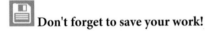 **Don't forget to save your work!**

Switching on the baseline grid

You can improve the layout of text with a publication by switching
on PagePlus's baseline grid feature. This ensures the horizontal
alignment of text is consistent across the page, regardless of text
position or size.

To switch on the baseline grid:

1. From the **Tools** menu, select **Options**.

2. In the **Options** dialog:

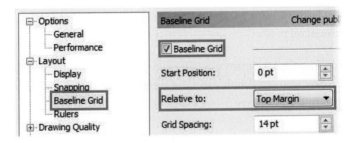

- Select the **Layout>Baseline Grid** sub-category on the left.

- Select the **Baseline Grid** option.

- From the **Relative to** drop-down list, select **Top Margin**.

- Click **OK**.

The baseline grid will appear across your publication's page.

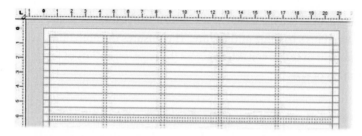

 For improved visibility, the baseline grid stops displaying if you zoom out of your publication passed 70% (by default). However, the baseline grid still remain active. This display threshold can be customized from the **Options** dialog.

We discuss working with the baseline grid in detail in the *Frame text* tutorial on p. 63.

You may find the many guidelines on your page distracting. If this is the case, you can simplify some of the guides by substituting them with ruler guides. We'll look at this next.

Don't forget to save your work!

Creating an asymmetrical grid using ruler guides

You can set up horizontal and vertical 'snap-to' ruler guides—non-printing, solid red lines that you can use to align headlines, pictures, and other layout elements.

There are two ways to create ruler guides:

- Automatically—in the **Ruler Guides** dialog. Use this method to place multiple ruler guides onto a page in precise positions.

  - or -

- Manually—by clicking and dragging on the rulers. Use this method to place individual ruler guides onto a page as you work.

We'll add ruler guides manually to set up an asymmetrical grid which we can then work to.

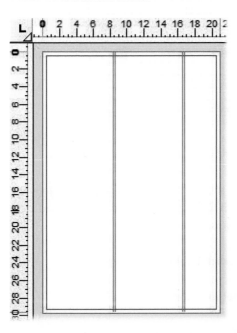

To create an asymmetrical grid

1. 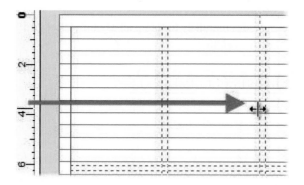 With your page set up as a 5 x 5 grid (as discussed on p. 23), on the **Hintline** toolbar, click **View Master Pages**.

2. Drag from the vertical ruler.

   A red line indicates the new ruler guide.

3. Position the ruler guide at the end of the second column.

4. Repeat the above two steps to place four ruler guides in total to mark the gaps between the second and third columns, and the fourth and fifth columns.

5. From the **File** menu, click **Publication Setup**.

6. In the **Publication Setup** dialog:

   • Select the **Margins** category on the left.

   • Set the number of **Rows** to 1.

- Set the number of **Columns** to 1.

- Click **OK**.

Your ruler guides marking the asymmetric grid will now appear on all pages which use the master page.

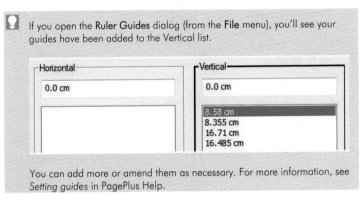

If you open the **Ruler Guides** dialog (from the **File** menu), you'll see your guides have been added to the Vertical list.

You can add more or amend them as necessary. For more information, see *Setting guides* in PagePlus Help.

 Don't forget to save your work!

Using spreads

Let's now explore some of the options in the **Publication Setup** dialog which will allow us to achieve this consistency in a longer publication.

To open a new publication and add additional pages:

1. From the **File** menu, click **Startup Assistant**.

2. On the left, click **New Publication**.

3. Click to select **A4** or **Letter** size paper.

4. From the **Insert** menu, click **Page**.

5. In the **Page Manager** dialog:

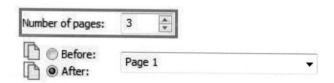

- In the **Number of pages** box, type **3**.

  Notice that we can also select where to add our pages. For example, if this were a multi-page publication, we could select **Before** or **After**, and then choose the page number from the drop-down list.

  We just have one page, so accept the default values (**After, Page 1**).

- Click **OK**.

The **Hintline** toolbar now displays '2 of 4' indicating that you are currently working on page two of a four page publication.

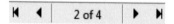

To set up spread/facing pages:

1. From the **File** menu, click **Publication Setup**.

2. In the **Publication Setup** dialog:

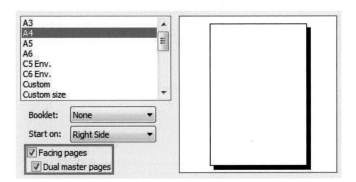

- Select the **Paper** category on the left.

- To set up the page layout as facing pages (also known as spreads), select the **Facing pages** option.

- To set up dual master pages (allowing you to run elements across the spread in the background of the publication, or position left- and right-side page numbers (see the *Creating a printed folded booklet* tutorial on p. 99)), select the **Dual master pages** option.

- Click **OK**.

If you're setting up a facing page layout where both left and right pages share the same master page, and you don't need to run background elements across the spread, clear the Dual master pages option.

You will now see a double-page spread—pages two and three of your publication. This is indicated on the **Hintline** toolbar by '2,3 of 4'.

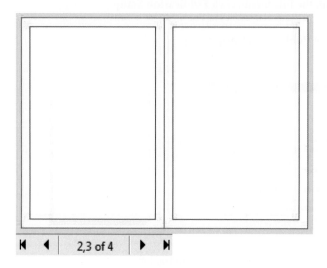

If you are producing a large publication which you intend to print and bind, you will need to adjust the page margins. To prevent content from disappearing into the bound publication's spine, you will need to set a wider margin on the right side of left (verso) pages and the left side of right (recto) pages. In other words, you need to set a wider inside margin. Let's look at this now.

To set page margins:

1. From the **File** menu, click **Publication Setup**.

2. In the **Publication Setup** dialog:

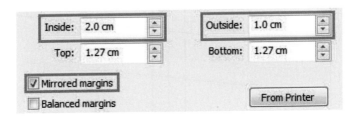

- Select the **Margins** category on the left.

- Ensure the **Mirrored margins** option is selected.

  This tells PagePlus to change the 'Left' margin setting to the 'Inside' margin, and the 'Right' margin to the 'Outside' margin on both facing pages.

- Set the **Inside page margin** to 2.00 cm.

- Set the **Outside page margin** to 1.00 cm.

3. If you intend on adding a header with page numbering, and book and chapter titles:

- Set the **Top page margin** to 2.00 cm.

- Set the **Bottom page margin** to 1.00 cm.

4. Click **OK**.

Your page margins update to reflect the settings in the dialog.

 Contrary to earlier discussions in this tutorial, you can place header content outside the top margin without affecting its printability. To ensure the header content does appear and page symmetry is maintained, you may wish to add a horizontal ruler guide to the master page spread positioned at 1 cm and work within this marker.

That's it! You now know how to work with a variety of guides to help you set out content on your page. All that's left is for you to add your content.

Don't forget to save your work!

Bleeds and scaling for professional printing

 10 min

If your publication is to be professionally printed, extending page elements beyond the trim edge and into bleed areas allows for inaccuracies in the trimming process and ensure your final publication looks perfect. We'll show you how to set up bleed guides to help in your design process and then walk you through setting a physical bleed area for professional PDF publication outputs.

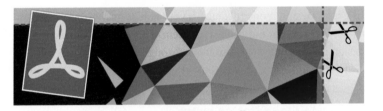

In this tutorial we'll set up a bleed of 0.3 cm (3 mm), however your professional printers may recommended setting a different width bleed. Contact your professional printers for more information.

By the end of this tutorial you will be able to:

- Set up bleed area guides.

- Apply a physical bleed area to a professional PDF output.

- Scale a publication during PDF output.

Let's begin...

1. From the **File** menu, click **Startup Assistant**.

2. On the left, click **New Publication**.

3. Click to select **A3** or **Tabloid** size paper.

   A single, blank page will open in the workspace.

Clean Design mode

In **Clean Design** mode (default), layout guides only display when an object is created or moved near to them. This is useful during the design process but, to help us work through this tutorial, we will switch Clean Design mode off to set up our publication.

To toggle Clean Design view:

• On the **Arrange** toolbar, click ⊞ **Clean Design**.

Setting up bleed area guides

Bleed area guides help you design your publication in preparation for professional printing. Let's set them up now, so you can see what they look like.

To set up bleed area guides:

1. From the **File** menu, select **Publication Setup**.

2. In the **Publication Setup** dialog:

   - Select the **Margins** category on the left.

   - In the **Bleed Guides** section, set the **Bleed area guides** (the 'trim edge' of the page) to 0.3 cm.

   - Click **OK**.

 The page border expands by the distance specified, and the trim edge is shown with dashed lines and scissors symbols.

Feel free to populate your page with your own content, using the bleed guides to extend objects beyond the trim edge.

 Still can't see your layout guides? From the View menu, ensure that Guide Lines and Bleed Area Guides are selected from the Grids and Guides flyout, and that Trimmed Mode is not selected.

Bleed area guides are visual aids only. If you want to add a physical bleed area to your printed publication, you will need to adjust your professional PDF output settings.

Save now! Click **File>Save As**, type in a new name and click **Save**.

Adding a physical bleed to a PDF

Although the bleed area guides on your page allow you to design with a trim edge, you'll still need to add a physical bleed area to your PDF output for your professional printers to work to. You can either use one of PagePlus's preset PDF profiles or manually set the bleed area.

To use a preset PDF profile:

1. On the **Standard** toolbar, click 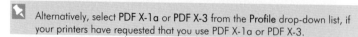 **Publish as PDF**.

2. In the **Publish PDF** dialog, from the **Profile** drop-down list, select **Press Ready**.

   The preview on the right updates to add a bleed area along with other prepress page marks.

   Alternatively, select PDF X-1a or PDF X-3 from the Profile drop-down list, if your printers have requested that you use PDF X-1a or PDF X-3.

3. Click **Publish**.

Your publication is published as a PDF using the selected preset profile.

To set up a custom bleed limit on a PDF output:

1. On the **Standard** toolbar, click 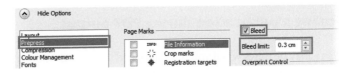 **Publish as PDF**.

2. In the **Publish PDF** dialog:

- Click  **More Options** to show advanced options (if not already displayed).

- Select the **Prepress** category on the left.

- Select the **Bleed** option and then, in the **Bleed limit** input box, type the amount you want to extend the printable area by. We set ours to 0.3 cm to match the bleed area guides we added earlier in this tutorial.

The preview updates to add your specified bleed area. The trim edge is indicated by the black border.

- Click **Publish**.

Your publication is published as a PDF using your custom settings.

 If your output includes Page Marks, the Bleed limit will automatically be adjusted (if necessary) so the selected page marks are entirely visible on the final print.

Scaling a publication during PDF output

There may be times when you have designed your publication at one page size but need to output it at another size. For example, at the last minute your club decides to produce A4 (Letter) rather than A3 (Tabloid) size posters. The scaling option in the **Publish PDF** dialog allows you to do this.

To scale a publication:

1. On the **Standard** toolbar, click **Publish as PDF**.

2. In the **Publish PDF** dialog:

   - Set the **Scale** to **70.1%** to create a PDF at one page size smaller than the design page size.

   - Set the **Scale** to **141.2%** to create a PDF at one page size larger than the design page size.

   - Click **Publish**.

Your publication is exported at one page size smaller or larger, depending on your scaling options. That's it! It's as easy as that to add bleeds and change the size of your publication during PDF output.

Designing stationery using Master pages and User Details

 20 min

Master pages allow you to share an underlying design across multiple publication pages. This allows you to achieve consistency throughout your publication, and save yourself a lot of time and effort in the process! We'll show you how to work with Master pages by creating letterhead stationery.

By the end of this tutorial you will be able to:

- Add pages to create a multiple page publication.

- Create a Master page.

- Assigning Master pages to pages.

- Save your publication as a template.

Let's begin...

1. From the **File** menu, click **Startup Assistant**.

2. On the left, click **New Publication**.

3. Click to select **A4** or **Letter** size paper.

    A single, blank page will open in the workspace.

Why use Master pages?

Master pages are like sheets of transparent paper located behind or in front of your main publication pages. Every page can have one or more Master pages assigned to it and a given Master page can be shared by any number of main pages.

When you add text frames, pictures, or other elements to the Master page, they appear in the same position on all publication pages that use that Master page.

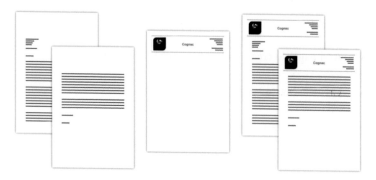

Typical elements that you'd place on a Master page include:

- background pictures (patterns, watermarks, etc.).

- page number using an automatic field (for more details, see the *Creating a printed folded booklet* tutorial on p. 99).

- company name, logo and/or contact details.

Master pages simplify publication maintenance as objects placed on a Master page only need updating once.

Adding publication pages

Currently we only have one page in our publication. Before we can show you the full power of Master pages, we need to add additional pages to our publication.

To add additional pages:

1. From the **Insert** menu, click **Page**.

2. In the **Page Manager** dialog:

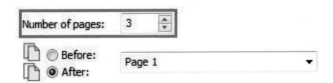

- In the **Number of pages** box, type **3**.

Notice that we can also select where to add our pages. For example, if this were a multi-page publication, we could select **Before** or **After**, and then choose the page number from the drop-down list.

We just have one page, so accept the default values (**After**, **Page 1**).

- Click **OK**.

The **Hintline** toolbar now displays '2 of 4' indicating that you are currently working on page two of a four page publication.

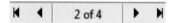

Creating a Master page (MasterA)

Now we have multiple publication pages, we'll show you how to access and design a Master page.

To access Master pages:

1. On the **Pages** tab, click **Master Pages** to show the Master Pages pane.

2. Double-click **MasterA** page thumbnail to display the page in the workspace.

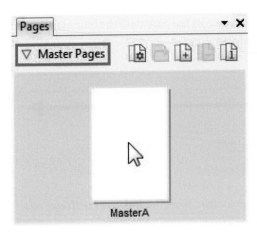

The page in the workspace resembles an ordinary page. However, any objects which are placed on this page will automatically appear on every page in your publication.

Let's try this out by adding a couple of basic straight lines.

To add lines to a page:

1. On the **Tools** toolbar, select the **Straight Line Tool**.

2. Position your cursor on the left side of the page where the blue margin guide appears.

3. Drag horizontally across the page until the blue margin guide on the right side appears.

To get a perfectly horizontal line by constraining the line's angle, hold down the Shift key as you drag.

4. On the **Colours** toolbar, from the ⬜ ▾ **Line** flyout, select **Scheme Colour 2**.

The Colours toolbar will remember the last Fill, Line and Text colour selected so you can quickly apply identical colours later in your project.

5. On the **Transform** tab, set the **Y** position to **5.3 cm**.

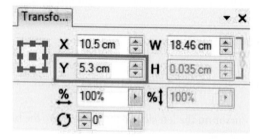

6. Repeat steps 2-4 to add a second straight line to your page.

7. On the **Tools** toolbar, select the **Pointer Tool**.

8. Drag the second line to the top of the page and position it over the top margin.

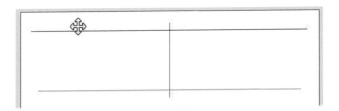

You now have two neat lines on your Master page.

Next we'll add some artistic text to our Master page design.

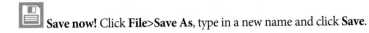 **Save now!** Click **File>Save As**, type in a new name and click **Save**.

To add and align artistic text:

1. On the **Tools** toolbar, click the **A** **Artistic Text Tool**.

2. Click between the previously added straight lines.

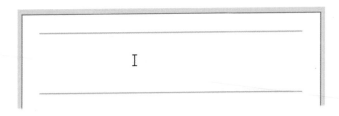

3. On the context toolbar, from the **Style** drop-down list, select **Heading 1**.

4. From the **Insert** menu, select **Information>User Details**.

5. In the **User Details** dialog, select **(Business) Company** and click **OK**.

6. **A** ▾ Click the border of the artistic text object (it will turn solid), then on the **Colours** toolbar, from the **Text** flyout, select **Scheme Colour 2**.

7. On the **Align** tab, click ⊡ **Centre Horizontally**.

8. Press **Ctrl+A** to select all three objects on the page.

9. On the **Align** tab, click ⊟ **Space Evenly Down**.

Your Master page should now resemble ours...

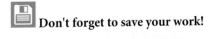

Don't forget to save your work!

Let's add our contact details to the header on the Master page too, using frame text.

To add user details as frame text:

1. On the **Tools** toolbar, click **Standard Text Frame**.

2. Position the cursor to the right of the company name and click once.

    A text frame is added at the default size.

3. From the **Insert** menu, select **Information>User Details**.

4. In the **User Details** dialog, select **(Business) Address Line 1** and click **OK**.

5. Press **Shift-Return** to add a soft return after the Address Line 1 user detail.

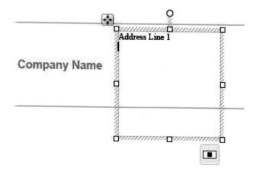

6. Repeat steps 3-5 to add address lines 2, 3, and 4.

7. Press the **Return** key after adding Address Line 4.

8. Repeat steps 3-5 to add **(Business) Phone** and **(Business) Web Site URL**.

Your Master page should now resemble ours...

Now let's neaten our contact details to ensure the header looks smart.

To align and update frame text:

1. Click to select the text frame and then drag the bottom central handle upwards to reduce the height of the text frame.

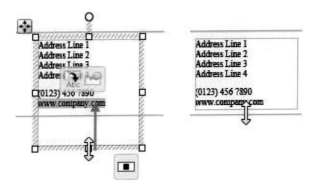

2. Click the border of the text frame (it will turn solid) and then:

   • On the **Colours** toolbar, from the $\underline{\mathbf{A}}$ ⁃ **Text** flyout, select **Scheme Colour 1**.

   • On the context toolbar, select ▤ **Right-align paragraph**.

   Alternatively, you can create and use a text style to format your contact details. For more information, see the *Text styles* tutorial on p. 87.

3. Drag the text frame's ✛ move button to the right to position the text frame closer to the page edge.

4. On the **Layers** tab:

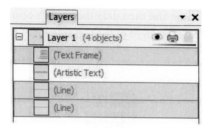

- Click ⊞ to expand **Layer 1** and display its contents.

- Press the **Ctrl** key and then select the **Text Frame** and the two **Line** objects.

5. On the **Align** tab, click 🔲 **Space Evenly Down**.

Your Master page should now resemble ours...

Remember, it's not only text you can add to a Master page. You can add any objects which appear on normal pages. To complete our Master page design we added a logo to our header (see opposite page).

Before we continue further with Master pages, let's divert for a moment to update our user details so we're no longer working with placeholder details.

Don't forget to save your work!

Updating user details

Modifying any (or all) of the user details in your publication can be done quickly in the User Details dialog.

To update user details:

1. From the **Tools** menu, click **Set User Details**.

2. In the **User Details** dialog, make any necessary changes and click **Update**.

These changes will immediately update on your publication.

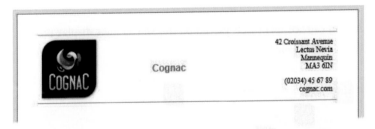

Depending on the length of your custom user details, you may have to modify the position of some of your text objects. As you can see the default company name was longer than our company, Cognac, so we will need to reposition this object.

Any changes to the **User Details** are saved globally and will update all existing and future publications containing User Details fields.

You may wish to take advantage of **Business Sets** which allow you to store variations of user details. For more information, see *Creating business sets* in PagePlus Help.

Now we'll return to Master pages and see how our creation interacts with other publication pages!

Assigning Master pages

By default, all publication pages automatically inherit MasterA as their Master page.

To view standard pages:

1. On the **Pages** tab, on the Pages pane, double-click a standard, publication page thumbnail.

2. Click through pages on the **Pages** tab, or click the arrows on the **Hintline** toolbar, to view the pages.

As you can see, all objects placed on the Master page display on all the standard pages.

This Master page works excellently as an opening page, but consider a four page correspondence—the full letterhead is extravagant on all pages.

Instead, we can create a second Master page which would better suit pages two onwards.

To create a second Master page:

1. On the **Pages** tab, on the Master Pages pane, double-click the 'MasterA' page thumbnail to display the page in the workspace.

2. Click **Master Page Manager**.

3. In the **Master Page Manager** dialog:

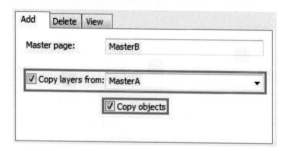

- Select the **Add** tab.

- Select **Copy layers from** and choose **Master A** from the drop-down list.

- Ensure the **Copy objects** option is selected.

- Click **OK**.

A new Master page, **MasterB**, is displayed in the workspace and as a thumbnail in the **Pages** tab.

If you have landscape and portrait pages in your publication, you can change the orientation of a Master page to match.

• On the **Pages** tab, on the Master Pages pane, select the appropriate Master page thumbnail.

• Click **Change Page Orientation**. The Master page updates.

You can now update the design to suit your needs.

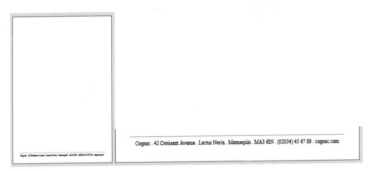

We created a footer using one of the straight lines and changed the layout of the user details to sit on a single line.

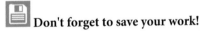 **Don't forget to save your work!**

We'll now walk you through applying these Master pages to publication pages.

To apply a Master page to all pages:

- On the **Pages** tab, on the Master Pages pane, right-click **MasterB** page thumbnail and select **Apply to>All pages**.

MasterB is applied to all publication pages on top of MasterA. This
demonstrates how you can stack up multiple Master pages on a
single standard page.

> If you have multiple Master pages on a single publication page where Master
> page elements overlap, the stacking order is important. The stacking order of
> Master pages can be modified from the **Layers** tab.

For the purposes of this tutorial, we only want one Master page per
publication page. MasterA applied to the first page and MasterB to
all others.

First, we'll remove MasterA from all pages.

To remove a Master page from publication pages:

- On the **Pages** tab, on the Master Pages pane, right-click
  MasterA page thumbnail and select **Apply to>None**.

Next, we'll remove all remaining Master pages from the first page.

To remove Master pages from a single publication page:

- On the **Pages** tab, on the Pages pane, right-click the page **1 of 4** thumbnail and select **Remove Master Pages**.

Finally, we'll reassign MasterA to the first page.

To assign a Master page to a single page:

- On the **Pages** tab, drag **MasterA** page thumbnail from the Master Pages pane and drop it on top of the **1 of 4** page thumbnail on the Pages pane.

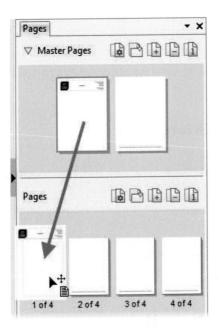

MasterA is now applied to the first page only, while all other
publication pages use MasterB.

You can confirm this set up by checking the page identifiers via the
Pages tab.

To check Master page assignment:

1. On the **Pages** tab, on the Pages pane, click **Page Identifiers**.

The assigned Master pages are displayed on each page thumbnail.

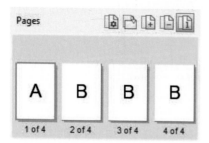

2.   Click the button again to return to the normal thumbnail view.

That's it! You have successfully created and assigned multiple
Master pages to a publication.

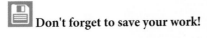   **Don't forget to save your work!**

Save as Template

Once you have your Master page design perfected, why not save the
publication as a template? You can then use the template as a
starting point for creating posters, flyers, events programmes,
letterheads, newsletters, and much more.

To save a publication as a template:

1. From the **File** menu click **Save As**.

2. In the **Save As** dialog, from the **Save as type** drop-down list, select **PagePlus Template (*.ppx)**.

   The dialog will automatically redirect to the **My Templates** sub-folder of your PagePlus X8 AppData folder. We recommend you save the template in this location.

3. Click **Save**.

If you save your file to the **My Templates** folder, you will be able to open publications using your template via the **New Publication** section of the **Startup Assistant**.

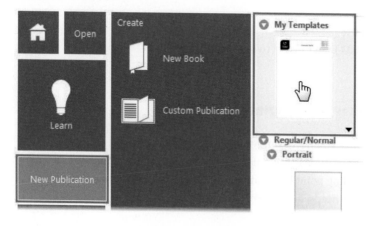

Frame text

 25 min

Text frames allow you to layout text on your page to help with the readability of your publication. We'll explore some of the unique properties of text frames to ensure you have all the necessary tools to build a successful publication.

By the end of this tutorial you will be able to:

- Create text frames.

- Create placeholder text.

- Link story text between frames.

- Work with frame columns.

- Align text with a baseline grid.

Let's begin...

1. From the **File** menu, click **Startup Assistant**.

2. On the left, click **New Publication**.

3. Click to select **A4** or **Letter** size paper.

A single, blank page will open in the workspace.

Alternatively...

- Open your saved publication/template from the *Designing stationery using Master pages and User Details* tutorial on p. 41, as we have.

About frame text

PagePlus provides two types of text—**frame text** and **artistic text**. Frame text is placed on the page inside a text frame, and is generally used for general copy, longer passages of text or non-decorative text such as contact details, product information, etc.

Artistic text is most often used for titles and decorative text.

Frame text has several special properties. It enables you to:

- Flow text between linked frames.

- Wrap text around pictures and shapes.

- Shape the frame to page objects.

- Implement padding, margins, and columns (both symmetrical and asymmetrical).

- Conform text layout to a baseline grid on an individual frame basis.

We'll look at some of these properties in this tutorial, but first we need to add a text frame and populate it with text.

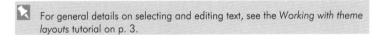

For general details on selecting and editing text, see the *Working with theme layouts* tutorial on p. 3.

To create a new text frame:

1. On the **Tools** toolbar, click **⬚** **Standard Text Frame**.

2. Move the cursor across the page until the blue page margin appears on the left side.

3. Drag across and down the page until two additional blue page margins appear.

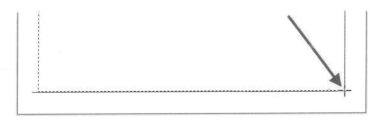

4.   The frame is created when you release the mouse button.

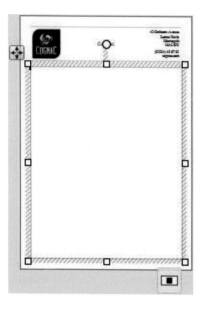

With our frame in place, let's add some text to it so we can visualize the properties of text frames.

To create placeholder text:

1.   The text frame should be selected and display a flashing text insertion cursor. If not, click on the page where the text frame is located.

2.   From the **Insert** menu, click **Fill with Placeholder Text** (or press **F5**).

The text frame is instantly filled with text which approximates the layout of publication text.

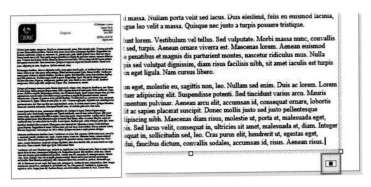

Notice the frame displays a **No Overflow** button, indicating that all of the story text is displayed.

Save now! Click **File>Save As**, type in a new name and click **Save**.

Linked frames

In PagePlus, you can link multiple text frames. This allows the text to flow from one frame to another automatically. We'll walk you through the process of linking frames next.

To resize a text frame:

1. The text frame should be selected and display a flashing text insertion cursor. If not, click on the page where the text frame is located.

2. Drag the right middle handle to inwards to reduce the width of the text frame.

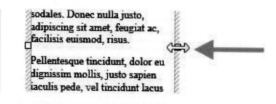

> You may wish to reduce the text frame to conform to column guides set on your publication. For more information, see the *Creating page layouts* tutorial on p. 19.

As your text frame decreases in size, you will notice the text flow indicators will update.

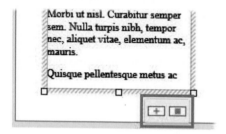

These two different buttons, ⊞ **AutoFlow** and ▣ **Overflow**, show that the frame contains more story text than can be displayed in the frame. We can ensure our text displays by creating new text frames for the text to flow into.

We can align these new text frames with our first text frame using dynamic guides.

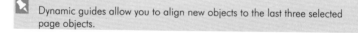

> Dynamic guides allow you to align new objects to the last three selected page objects.

To use dynamic guides:

- On the **Arrange** toolbar:

- Ensure **Snapping** is enabled.

- From the **Snapping** flyout, ensure **Dynamic Guides** is enabled.

Now, we'll create a new text frame and link the story text.

To link existing text frames:

1. On the **Tools** toolbar, click **Standard Text Frame**.

2. Move the cursor across the page until a red dynamic guide appears when the cursor is in line with the first text frame.

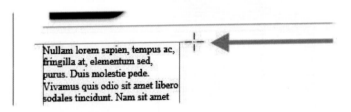

3. Drag across and down the page until the bottom blue page margins appear. Aim for the second text frame to fill the remainder of the page.

4. Click inside the left text frame containing the text.

The ⊞ **AutoFlow** and ▣ **Overflow** buttons are displayed.

5. Click the ▣ **Overflow** button.

The cursor will change to ▶▯🗐 .

6. Hover over the new text frame and click once when the edges glow.

The text flows into the new frame, which is now linked to the first frame.

Notice that a ▼ **Continued (Overflow)** button is displayed. This indicates that the frame is now linked, but that the last frame in the sequence still contains overflow text.

Click inside the second frame. As you can see, the **AutoFlow** and **Overflow** buttons are still available, meaning that the linked frames still contain additional text. We'll flow the text into a new frame on a new page all in one procedure!

To create a linked text frame:

1. Click inside the second text frame and then click the **Overflow** button.

    The cursor will change to .

2. On the **Hintline** toolbar, click **Next Page**.

    If you began this tutorial from a new publication, in the **Page Manager** dialog:

    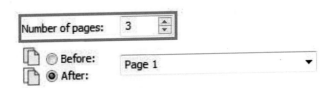

    - In the **Number of pages** box, type **3**.

    - Click **OK**.

3. Move the cursor across the page until the blue page margin appears on the left and top side.

4. Drag across and down the page to create a text frame which fills the page.

   The linked frame is created when you release the mouse button, and is filled with the overflowing story text from the previous frames.

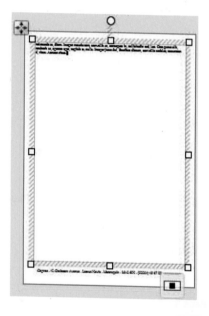

Notice that the frame now displays a 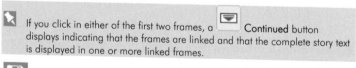 **No Overflow** button, indicating that all of the story text is now displayed.

> If you click in either of the first two frames, a 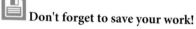 **Continued** button displays indicating that the frames are linked and that the complete story text is displayed in one or more linked frames.

Don't forget to save your work!

Working with text frame columns

In the previous example, we created a column layout using linked frames. However, a single frame can have multiple columns. This can help simplify the layout design as it takes the worry out of aligning multiple frames. Let's look at this now.

To change the frame layout:

1. The text frame should be selected and display a flashing text insertion cursor. If not, click on the page where the text frame is located.

2. From the **Insert** menu, click **Fill with Placeholder Text** (or press **F5**).

   This will fill the remaining space with more placeholder text.

3. On the context toolbar, set the column number to **2**.

The text frame updates to contain two columns.

By default, columns are symmetrical. However, you can create an asymmetrical design (like our first page) via the **Frame Properties** dialog.

To create asymmetrical columns:

1. 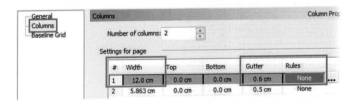 With the text frame still selected, on the context toolbar, click **Text Frame Properties**.

2. In the **Frame Properties** dialog:

#	Width	Top	Bottom	Gutter	Rules
1	12.0 cm	0.0 cm	0.0 cm	0.6 cm	None
2	5.863 cm	0.0 cm	0.0 cm	0.5 cm	None

General
Columns
Baseline Grid

Columns   Column Pro

Number of columns: 2

Settings for page

- Select the **Columns** category on the left.

- Set the **Width** for the first column (furthest to the left) to **12 cm**.

- Set the **Gutter** for the first column to **0.6 cm**.

- In the **Rules** column, click **None**.

- In the **Line and Border** dialog, from the **Style** drop-down list, select a line style and click **OK**.

3. Back in the **Frame Properties** dialog, select the **Mirror settings for left and right pages** option.

4. Click **OK**.

The text frame updates to give two asymmetrical columns with a dividing line between.

However, what about the final attribute we applied? The mirror settings options comes into play when our publication is set up as a spread (facing pages).

 Don't forget to save your work!

To set up spread/facing pages:

1. From the **File** menu, click **Publication Setup**.

2. In the **Publication Setup** dialog:

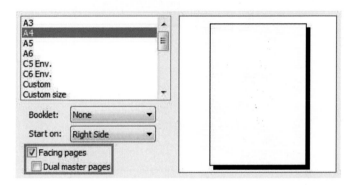

- Select the **Pages** category on the left.

- To set up the page layout as facing pages (also known as spreads), select the **Facing pages** option.

- Ensure the **Dual master pages** option is not selected.

- Click **OK**.

You will now see a double-page spread—pages two and three of your publication—as indicated in the **Hintline** toolbar.

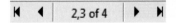

Now we'll move the frame text to the other page...

To move a text frame:

- Drag the text frame's move button to the right to position the text frame on the right (recto) page.

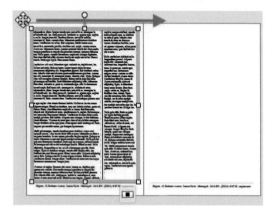

As you move the text frame to the right, the frame's properties are mirrored, resulting in an inverted asymmetric layout.

The frame's properties will also be mirrored if an additional page is added to the publication preceding the page on which the text frame is located.

Baseline grid

In this final section, we'll explore how text within a frame interacts with the baseline grid. First, though, we need to set up another page of text.

To create another page of text:

1. On the **Hintline** toolbar, click ▶ **Next Page** to display page 4.

2. Add one narrow and another wider text frame to the page and fill them both with placeholder text but do not link them.

Your page should now resemble ours...

Now let's set up our baseline grid.

To switch on the baseline grid:

1. From the **Tools** menu, select **Options**.

2. In the **Options** dialog:

- Select the **Layout>Baseline Grid** sub-category on the left.

- Select the **Baseline Grid** option.

- Click **OK**.

The baseline grid will appear across your publication's page. All the text on the page shifts to align to the baseline grid.

| Vivamus vel sapien. Praesent nisl tortor, laoreet eu, dapibus quis, egestas non, mauris. Cum sociis natoque penatibus et magnis dis | Maecenas condimentum tincidunt lorem. Vestibulum vel tellus. Sed vulputate. Morbi massa nunc, convallis a, commodo gravida, tincidunt sed, turpis. Aenean ornare viverra est. Maecenas lorem. Aenean euismod iaculis dui. Cum sociis natoque penatibus et magnis dis |

For improved visibility, the baseline grid stops displaying if you zoom out of your publication passed 70% (by default). However, the baseline grid still remain active. This display threshold can be customized from the Options dialog.

Alignment to the baseline grid is controlled by text paragraph settings. Therefore, each paragraph within your publication can be set to align or not, as you choose. However, it is more likely you will want entire stories to align or not. We recommend using text styles to achieve this.

For more information on working with text styles, see the *Text styles* tutorial on p. 87.

To update a text style:

I. Click anywhere in either text frame.

On the **Text Styles** tab, you will see the text is set to the **Body** paragraph text style.

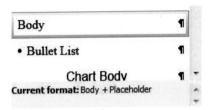

2. On the **Text Styles** tab, right-click **Body** and select **Modify Body**.

3. In the **Text Style** dialog:

• Select the **Paragraph>Alignment and Spacing** sub-category on the left.

Notice the **Align to baseline grid** option is selected for this text style. This is why our frame text aligned itself automatically.

If this option is switched off, text using this style will not align to the baseline grid.

- To continue with the tutorial, leave the **Align to baseline grid** option selected and click **OK**.

Now, let's see what happens if we change the size of the text in the left frame and how this affects the layout.

To change text size:

1. Click anywhere in the left text frame and then press **Ctrl+A** to select all the text.

2. On the context toolbar, change the **Point Size** to **8 pt**.

   The text shrinks but still aligns to the baseline grid. This ensures it is also still aligned to the text in the right frame.

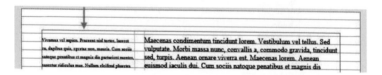

3. Repeat step 1 and then change the **Point Size** to **18 pt**.

   Alignment to the baseline is still maintained.

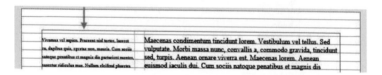

Although the text in the two frames still align, you may not be happy with the line spacing in the left text frame. If this is the case, you can always enable a baseline grid for that text frame alone! We'll show you how.

To set up a unique text frame baseline grid:

1. 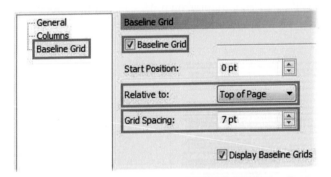 With the text frame still selected, on the context toolbar, click **Text Frame Properties**.

2. In the **Frame Properties** dialog:

General	Baseline Grid		
Columns	☑ Baseline Grid		
Baseline Grid	Start Position:	0 pt	⬍
	Relative to:	Top of Page ▼	
	Grid Spacing:	7 pt	⬍
		☑ Display Baseline Grids	

- Select the **Baseline Grid** category on the left.

- Select the **Baseline Grid** option.

- From the **Relative to** drop-down list, select **Top of Page**.

- Set the **Grid Spacing** to half the size of the publication-wide spacing. In this case, **7 pt**.

- Click **OK**.

The text in the frame aligns to its own unique baseline grid, thereby reducing the line spacing.

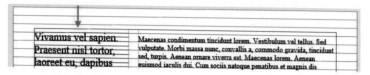

However, because the line spacing was still in proportion to the publication-wide baseline grid spacing, all the text still aligns correctly.

If you have been following along with this tutorial using your saved publication/template from the *Designing stationery using Master pages and User Details* tutorial on p. 41, you may have noticed the footer text has 'disappeared'.

This is because the footer used the Body text style and by aligning the style with the baseline grid, it has forced the text off the page. We'll show you how you can rectify this on an individual paragraph basis.

To remove alignment to baseline grid:

1. On the **Pages** tab, click **Master Pages** to show the Master Pages pane.

2. Double-click **MasterB** page thumbnail to display the page in the workspace.

3. Select the text frame at the bottom of the page and then press **Ctrl+A** to select all the text.

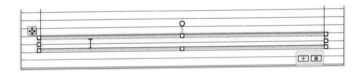

4. On the **Paragraph** tab, ensure the **Align to Baseline Grid** option is not selected.

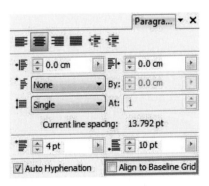

The text has reappeared as this selected paragraph no longer aligns to the baseline grid.

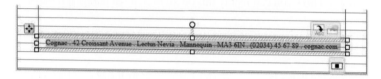

That's it! Now you know how to work with text frames and some of its many properties to ensure your publications look stunning.

 Don't forget to save your work!

Text styles

 15 min

A text style is a set of character and/or paragraph attributes saved as a group. When you apply a style to text, you apply the whole group of attributes in just one step. The **Text Styles** tab contains pre-defined text styles you can quickly apply to text. In this tutorial, we'll look at applying and modifying preset styles.

By the end of this tutorial you will be able to:

- Use Page assets to quickly set up a publication.

- Apply text styles throughout a publication.

- Modify individual and multiple text styles.

- Reassign text styles to change the look and layout of text instantly.

Let's begin...

1. From the **File** menu, click **Startup Assistant**.

2. On the left, click **New Publication**.

3. Click to select **A4** or **Letter** size paper.

   A single, blank page will open in the workspace.

Using the tutorial Page Content asset

To help us progress with this tutorial together, we have provided a short book entitled *Self-publish Your Own eBook* which can be found in the **Tutorials** assets pack.

To add tutorial assets to the Assets tab:

1. On the **Assets** tab, click **Browse** to open the **Asset Browser**.

2. In the **Pack Files** section, select the **Tutorials** pack.

3. In the **Page Content** category, click the **Book** text frame. (Names appear as tooltips.)

The green 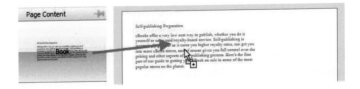 shows that it has been added to the tab.

4. Click **Close** to exit.

The asset is added to the Page Content category in the Assets tab.

To add page content to the page:

1. On the **Assets** tab, the **Page Content** category should be displayed (if not, click the **Page Content** header).

2. Drag the page content asset to the page.

3. Drag the text frame's ⊕ move button to position the text frame using the top and left page margins.

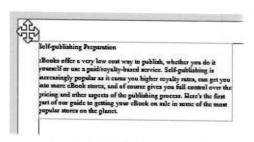

4. Drag the bottom right handle downwards to resize the text frame so it fills most of the page—you can use the blue margin lines that appear to help you place your frame.

The Page Content asset consists of a single text frame containing our book.

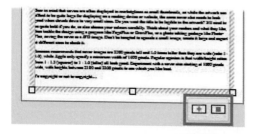

There is too much content for just a single frame, as indicated by the buttons at the bottom of the frame. So we need to create some more text frames to accommodate the publication's text. We can do this using **AutoFlow**.

To autoflow text:

1. With the text frame still selected, click 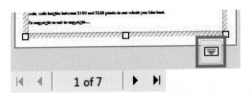 **AutoFlow**.

2. If the **Select Autoflow Frame Attributes** dialog displays, select either option and click **OK**.

PagePlus automatically creates new text frames on new pages within your publication to accommodate the entire publication.

You will notice the frame's button has changed to indicate there is more text which flows into additional text frames. There are also more pages in the publication (see the **Hintline** toolbar).

Now we'll update this publication using text styles.

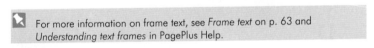

For more information on frame text, see *Frame text* on p. 63 and *Understanding text frames* in PagePlus Help.

Save now! Click **File>Save As**, type in a new name and click **Save**.

Applying text styles

We will use the pre-designed text styles which come with PagePlus. These are available within all new publications. In particular, we'll concentrate on Heading 1, Heading 2, and Heading 3, to establish a hierarchical structure within our book.

First we'll establish the beginning of a chapter by using Heading 1.

To apply a Heading 1 style:

1. With the text frame selected, drag to select the first sentence, 'Self-publishing Preparation'

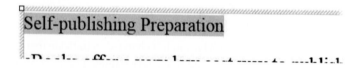

2. On the **Text Styles** tab, click **Heading 1**.

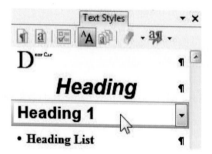

The text updates to adopt the selected style.

Self-publishing Preparation
~~eRooks offer a very low cost way to publish~~

Next, we'll establish paragraph titles as the next step down in the hierarchy by setting them to Heading 2.

> Heading 2 style will display in the Text Styles tab automatically once Heading 1 style is applied to text within your publication. Heading 3 will appear once Heading 2 has been applied, and so on. You can, however, view all available styles by clicking **Show All** on the **Text Styles** tab.

To apply a Heading 2 style:

1. With the text frame selected, drag to select 'Are you prepared?'.

   ### Are you prepared?
   ~~There's more than writing required of you -~~

2. On the **Text Styles** tab, click **Heading 2**.

   ### *Are you prepared?*
   There's more than writing required of you -

   The text updates to adopt the selected style.

Continue to apply Heading text styles throughout the publication. We recommend setting 'Publishing your eBook', 'Publishing on Amazon', and 'References' as Heading 1. We'd also recommend setting the paragraph titles 'In the USA', 'In the UK', and 'Other territories' to Heading 3.

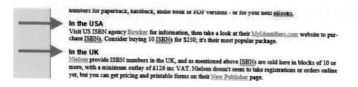

Now, let's look at how easy it is to update these applied styles to change the look of our publication.

Modifying text styles

If the default PagePlus preset text styles don't suit your specific needs, you can change them in several ways. If these styles are already applied to publication text, once the style has been updated, all text using that style is instantly updated. Let's see how this works.

To modify a single text style:

1. On the **Text Styles** tab, right-click **Heading 2** and select **Modify Heading 2**.

2. In the **Text Style** dialog:

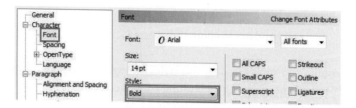

- Select the **Character>Font** sub-category on the left.

- From the **Style** drop-down list, select **Bold** and click **OK**.

The modified style is applied to all text in the publication using Heading 2 style.

Now let's look at a situation where you wish to change the font of all the Heading styles. Rather than modifying each style independently as we did above, we can modify the parent style and the change will appear in all its children.

To modify a parent text style:

1. On the **Text Styles** tab, click 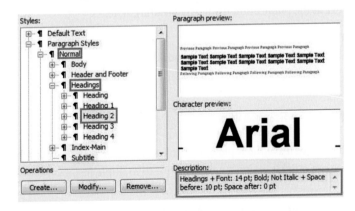 **Manage**.

You can clearly see the hierarchy inherent in the text styles in the current publication. Heading 2 is based on Headings which itself is based on Normal. As all our applied heading styles use the Headings parent style, by updating the Headings style we will affect all of the heading styles.

2. In the **Text Styles Palette** dialog, select **Headings** and click **Modify**.

3. In the **Text Style** dialog:

   * Select the **Character>Font** sub-category on the left.

   * From the **Font** drop-down list, select **Trebuchet MS**.

   * Click **OK**.

4. In the **Text Styles Palette** dialog, click **Close**.

All Heading styles are updated using the new font and applied to all text in the publication using any Heading style.

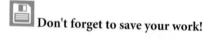 **Don't forget to save your work!**

Reassigning text styles

Before we leave the topic of text styles, let's look at the way in which we can quickly assign a new text style to multiple instances of text.

To change text throughout a publication:

1. Follow the procedure *To modify a parent text style* on the previous page to set the **Normal** font to **Tahoma**.

2. On the **Text Styles** tab:

- Right-click **Body eBook** and select **Select All Instance(s)**.

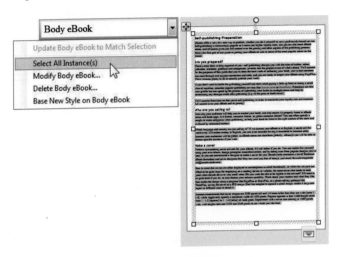

All paragraphs with Body eBook text style applied are selected throughout the publication.

- Click **Body**.

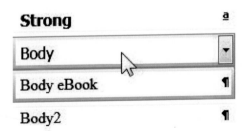

As the Body text style is based on the Normal parent style, all selected paragraphs immediately update to use Tahoma font as well as additional paragraph styles.

That's it! Now you know how to work with text styles to help with the design of publications.

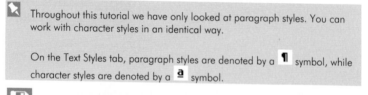

Throughout this tutorial we have only looked at paragraph styles. You can work with character styles in an identical way.

On the Text Styles tab, paragraph styles are denoted by a 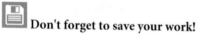 symbol, while character styles are denoted by a ⁢ symbol.

Don't forget to save your work!

Creating a printed folded booklet

 45 min

Creating a printed folded booklet using PagePlus and your desktop printer allows you to distribute information about your company, club, or charity with ease without involving external parties or professional printers. In this tutorial, we'll walk you through adding a table of contents and page numbering to a publication, before printing it in the form of a handy size booklet.

 We're going to use a blank publication for this tutorial. However, you can undertake the steps for a publication which has already been written and edited.

By the end of this tutorial you will be able to:

- Generate a table of contents from applied text styles.

- Modify a table of contents.

- Add and amend page numbering.

- Remove page numbering from an individual page.

- Imposing and printing a publication as a folded booklet.

Let's begin...

1. From the **File** menu, click **Startup Assistant**.

2. On the left, click **New Publication**.

3. Click to select **A4** or **Letter** size paper.

   A single, blank page will open in the workspace.

To help us progress with this tutorial together, we have provided a short book entitled *Self-publish Your Own eBook* which can be found in the **Tutorials** assets pack. However, feel free to complete the tutorial using a book you have already written in, or imported into, PagePlus.

To add tutorial assets and text styles:

- Follow the *Using the tutorial Page Content asset* (p. 88) and *Applying text styles* (p. 92) procedures outlined in the *Text styles* tutorial and then continue with this tutorial.

Now we have some text styles applied to our publication, let's generate our table of contents!

 Don't forget to save your work!

Generating a table of contents

We'll add a table of contents to the first page of our publication. However, to help us organize the project neatly, we'll add the table of contents to a blank text frame on a newly created page.

To add a new page:

- 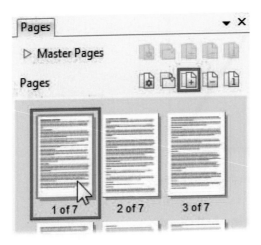 On the **Pages** tab, click the first page and then click **Add Page**.

A new page is added to your publication before page 1, and is displayed in the workspace.

To add a text frame:

1. On the **Tools** toolbar, click  **Standard Text Frame**.

2. Drag to create a text frame which fills most of the page—you can use the blue margin lines that appear to help you place your frame.

Now, let's add our table of contents.

To insert a table of contents:

1. With your new, blank text frame still selected, from the **Insert** menu, select **Table of Contents**.

   The default text of 'Contents' is added at the top, centre of your text frame and the TOC tab displays.

2. On the **TOC** tab, select the check box to the left of **Heading 1**.

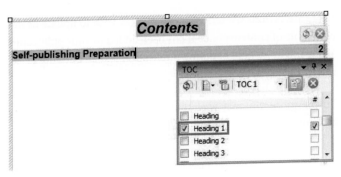

The table of contents automatically updates on the page to display any text with Heading 1 applied and the page number of the page it is located on.

3. On the **TOC** tab, select the check box to the left of **Heading 2**.

The table of contents automatically updates on the page to display any text with Heading 2 applied and the page number of the page it is located on.

When you add a table of contents to the page and then select the text style from the TOC tab, PagePlus analyzes your publication and lists every instance of the text style and the page number it appears on. Next we'll look at modifying a table of contents.

 Don't forget to save your work!

Modifying a table of contents

There are various scenarios when you may wish to update or modify your table of contents once it has been added to your publication. These might include updating publication text and adding or removing pages.

Furthermore, you may wish to include other Heading levels in your table of contents. We'll examine this scenario next...

To update table of contents:

1. On the **TOC** tab, select the check box to the left of **Heading 3**.

    The table of contents should automatically update to include sections with **Heading 3** applied (if not, on the **TOC** tab, click **Regenerate**).

    The Heading 3 titles list their page number, but as they are all on the same page and part of the 'Do you need an ISBN?' discussion, so let's remove the page numbers.

2. On the **TOC** tab, uncheck the box to the right of **Heading 3**.

The table of contents updates to display the Heading 3 sections but not their associated page numbers.

If further content is added to the publication, or content is removed, we recommend regenerating the table of contents. On the TOC tab, click **Regenerate**.

There may be occasions when you might want to change the text styles within your table of contents. We'll show you how you can modify these by reducing the spacing between the second and third levels of the table of contents (i.e. those sections with Heading 2 and Heading 3 applied).

To modify table of contents text styles:

1. From the **Tools** toolbar, select the **Pointer Tool**, and then, in the table of contents, click anywhere after **Are you prepared?**.

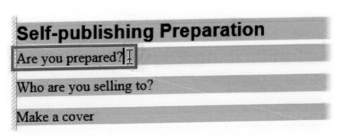

The Text Styles tab updates to display specific table of contents text styles (with a prefix of 'Contents-').

2. On the **Text Styles** tab, right-click **Contents-2nd** and then select **Modify Contents-2nd**.

3. In the **Text Styles** dialog:

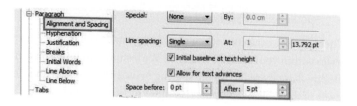

- Select the **Paragraph>Alignment and Spacing** sub-category on the left.

- Set the space **After** to **5pt**.

- Click **OK**.

The table of contents updates to reflect the new spacing of Contents-2nd.

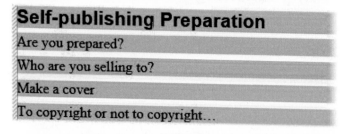

Contents-3rd text style is linked to Contents-2nd, so any changes made to Contents-2nd are reflected in Contents-3rd. You can update Contents-3rd independently by following steps 2 and 3 of the above procedure and selecting **Contents-3rd** instead.

You can add a 'tab leader' to your table of contents to help readers link the sections listed on the left with the page numbering listed on the right.

To add a tab leader:

*   On the **TOC** tab, click **Tab Leader** and select a leader style from the drop-down list.

    We selected a dotted leader style.

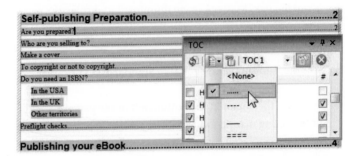

Now we have our table of contents in place and styled to our taste, let's add page numbers.

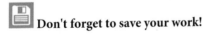 **Don't forget to save your work!**

Adding and amending page numbering

We can easily add page numbers to every page by simply adding them to the master page(s) of our publication. PagePlus does the rest! For more information on using master pages, see *Designing stationery using Master pages and User Details* on p. 41.

To add a page number to a master page:

1. On the **Pages** tab, click **Master Pages** to show the Master Pages pane.

   The publication currently has one master page which is applied to all pages.

2. Double-click 'MasterA' page thumbnail to display the page in the workspace.

3. On the **Tools** toolbar, click  **Standard Text Frame**.

4. Position the cursor at the bottom left of the page—two blue intersecting margin guides will appear.

5. Drag across and down the page until the blue margin guide appears on the right of the page.

   When you release the mouse button you'll see a flashing text-insertion cursor.

6. On the **Text Styles** tab, click **Show All** and then select **Footer**.

7. From the **Insert** menu, click **Information>Page Number**.

The automatic page number placeholder is inserted.

The actual number will correctly update when viewed on a page (and not the master page).

8. On the **Pages** tab, double-click each of the page thumbnails to display them in the workspace.

from 1 : 1.3 (squarer) to 1 : 1.6 (taller) all look good. Experiment with a cover size starting at 1600 pixels wide, with heights between 2100 and 2560 pixels to see which you like best.

2

Preflight checks
With your work written, images placed inline so they flow properly with your text, and your eBook proofed and polished, you'll be ready to output. Perform a final check in PagePlus and then create your file ready for publishing. Open your eBook publication in PagePlus and locate the Preflight tab. If it's hidden, display it by using the View > Studio Tabs menu. Choose ePub from the drop-down output choices and click Check. Note any recommendations or warnings, e.g. floating images that are not inline within your text, or chapters that exceed the size laid out in eBook standards.

3

As you can see, the page number is displayed in the same place at the bottom of each page.

You'll frequently see brochures, magazines, and books with page numbers which alternate between the left and right side of the page, depending on whether they display on a verso (left) or recto (right) page, respectively. This can be set up in PagePlus using facing pages and dual master pages.

To set up facing pages:

1. On the **File** menu, select **Publication Setup**.

2. In the **Publication Setup** dialog:

   - Select the **Pages** category on the left.

   - To set up the page layout as facing pages (also known as spreads), select the **Facing pages** option.

   - To set up dual master pages, select the **Dual master pages** option.

   - Click **OK**.

The Pages tab updates to display facing pages side-by-side in both the Pages and Master Pages window.

In the workspace your pages also display as a double-page spread.

Now we have facing pages and dual master pages, we can set up page numbering to alternate between left and right (verso and recto) pages.

To set up dual master pages:

1. Ensure 'MasterA' is displayed in the workspace (if not, double-click 'MasterA' thumbnail on the Master Pages pane of the **Pages** tab).

2. Click to select the text frame and then, while holding down the **Ctrl** key, drag the frame's ⊕ move button to the right page.

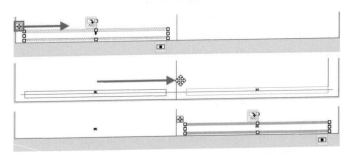

A copy of the frame is created as you drag.

💡 You can also hold down the Shift key to ensure the two frames stay aligned.

3. ☰ With the text frame on the right page still selected, on the context toolbar, select **Right-align Paragraph**.

4. ☰ Click to select the text frame on the left page and, on the context toolbar, select **Left-align Paragraph**.

5. On the **Pages** tab, double-click the **2,3 of 8** page thumbnail to display the facing pages in the workspace.

The pages now display alternating left to right page numbering.

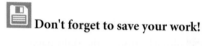 **Don't forget to save your work!**

Conventionally, the main content within a book or booklet begins on a right (recto) page and this is considered the first numbered page. Currently our main publication content starts on page two which is a left (verso) page. Let's make our publication more conventional!

To adopt a conventional booklet layout:

1. On the **Pages** tab, click the second page and then click **Add Page**.

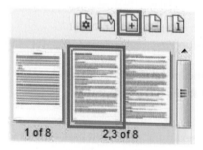

2. A new page is added to your publication between page 1 and 2, and is displayed in the workspace.

3. From the **Format** menu, select **Page Number Format**.

4. In the **Page Number Format** dialog:

> **Numbering**
>
> ☐ Continue from previous chapter
>
> First page number: -1

- Ensure the **Continue from previous chapter** option is not selected.

- Set the **First page number** to -**1**.

  This will set the first (table of contents), second (blank), and third (booklet text) physical pages to numbered pages -1, 0, and 1, respectively.

- Click **OK**.

The page numbers will vanish from the first two pages (PagePlus does not list page numbers below 1) and the third will be listed as page 1. This change is also reflected in the Pages tab by the numbers in parentheses.

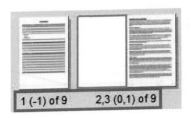

1 (-1) of 9   2,3 (0,1) of 9

You will also notice the table of contents has automatically updated to reflect the new pagination.

If your table of contents has not automatically updated, you can manually update it. On the **TOC** tab, click **Regenerate**.

Don't forget to save your work!

(Optional) Preparing for print

The procedures in this section are not essential for the successful printing of your booklet, but provide the ideal opportunity to refresh some of the procedures covered in this tutorial so far. If you wish to proceed to print immediately, see the *Printing a folded booklet* section below on p. 119.

Books should ideally be an even number of pages and, for folded booklets, a multiple of four. As you can see, our publication currently has an odd number of pages. Let's increase our page count from nine to 12 by creating a title page and ending on a blank page.

To add a new page:

1. On the **Pages** tab, click the first page and then click **Add Page**.

2. Repeat the above step to add another page.

We also need to update the pagination of our publication.

To change page number format:

1. From the **Format** menu, select **Page Number Format**.

2. In the **Page Number Format** dialog:

   - Set the **First page number** to **-3**.

   - Click **OK**.

Our new first page should be displayed in the workspace. Let's set up a title page for out publication.

To design a title page:

1. On the **Tools** toolbar, click  **Standard Text Frame**.

2. Click about a third of the way down your page to add a text frame at the default size.

3. On the **Align** tab, click **Centre Horizontally**.

4. On the **Text Styles** tab, click **Title**.

5. Type the title of the publication.

6. Press the **Return** key and, on the **Text Styles** tab, click **Subtitle**.

7. Type the name of the publication's author.

8. Feel free to add any additional information and reposition your objects as desired.

We added a logo at the bottom of the page to show the publisher.

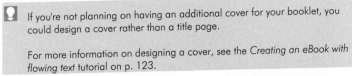

If you're not planning on having an additional cover for your booklet, you could design a cover rather than a title page.

For more information on designing a cover, see the *Creating an eBook with flowing text* tutorial on p. 123.

Now we'll add a final, blank page at the end of our publication.

To add a new page:

1. ▶ ▶ On the **Hintline** toolbar, click **Last Page** and then **Next Page**.

2. In the **Page Manager** dialog, click **OK**.

A new page is added to the end of the publication but the page number looks out of place. We can remove the page number by promoting it from master page and then deleting it.

To promote and delete an object from a master page:

1. Click to select the text frame at the bottom of the page.

   An object toolbar will appear on the text frame showing it is located on the master page.

2. Click ⌃A **Promote from Master Page**.

   The text frame will become detached from the master page for this page only. This is shown by the updated object toolbar.

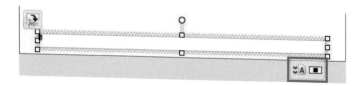

3. Click to select the text frame and then press the **Delete** key.

The page number is removed but every other page remains unaffected.

If you wish to remove the master page in its entirety from a standard page, in the **Pages** tab, right-click the page thumbnail and selecting **Remove Master Pages**. For more information on using master pages, see *Designing stationery using Master pages and User Details* on p. 41.

Now, let's print our publication as a folded booklet!

Printing a folded booklet

Our publication is currently set up as a regular, non-folding portrait publication. This can be seen by reviewing the Paper category of the Publication Setup dialog (**File>Publication Setup**).

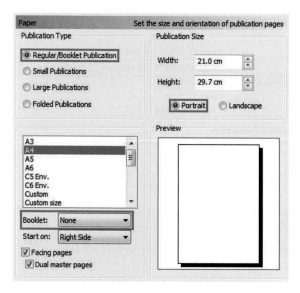

However, we want to produce a folded booklet which is half the current size. Printing directly from PagePlus will allow us to convert our publication as we go.

To preview the publication:

1. From the **File** menu, select **Print / PDF Preview**.

2. If you receive a message regarding your table of contents:

   - Click **Yes** to ensure it is up-to-date.

   - Click **No** if you have manually adjusted the table of contents and know it to be otherwise up-to-date.

3. If you receive a message about the sheet orientation, click **Yes**.

PagePlus will open your publication in **Preview** mode.

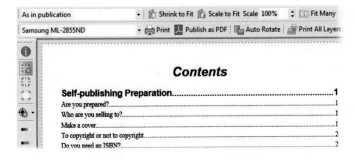

Preview mode is an excellent environment for print-time imposition of a publication. Not only are all the settings easily accessible, but the preview updates so you can see what the final production will look like before committing to print.

To set up the printing of a folded booklet:

1. On the **Printer** toolbar, from the **Select Printer** drop-down list, select a printer.

2. On the **Imposition** toolbar:

- From the **Imposition Mode** drop-down list, select **Side Fold Booklet**. If you receive a message about the sheet orientation, click **Yes**.

  The preview will update and you will notice the contents of pages do not display fully.

- Select  **Scale to Fit**.

  The preview will update to show your pages neatly displayed across the page as they will print.

3. On the **Margins** toolbar (at the bottom of Preview mode window), set the **Creep** to **0.1 cm**.

  This will leave more space between opposite sheets on outer leaves than on inner leaves to allow for pages which sit inside of others. For longer booklets, the Creep setting may need to be higher.

Feel free to click through the publication pages using the controls at the bottom left of the window to see how the booklet will print.

To print a folded booklet:

1. From the **File** menu, select **Print**.

2. In the **Print** dialog:

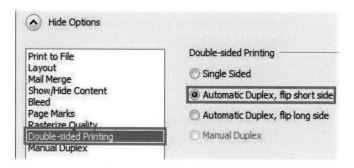

- Click ⌄ **More Options**.

- Select the **Double-sided Printing** category on the left and select an **Automatic Duplex** option. We chose the **flip short side** option but, as every printer is different, your printer may require the **flip long side** option.

  If your printer does not support double-sided (duplex) printing, you will need to set up **Manual Duplex**. For more information, see *Printing basics* in PagePlus Help.

- Click **Print**.

That's it! You have now successfully created and printed a booklet ready for folding.

Creating an eBook with flowing text

 40 min

In this tutorial, we'll take you through setting up a publication in preparation for creating an eBook, which can then be published online.

Publishing as eBooks in PagePlus Help provides tips and tricks on the best ways of creating and writing a book in PagePlus, if you're planning to publish it as an eBook. These include keeping your text within text frames and using text styles. We'll look at these in more detail in this tutorial.

By the end of this tutorial you will be able to:

- Set up your publication to create the best eBook layout.

- Add hyperlinks to your eBook.

- Create a cover for your eBook using assets.

- Export your publication to an EPUB 2 format.

Let's begin...

1. From the **File** menu, click **Startup Assistant**.

2. On the left, click **New Publication**.

3. Scroll down to the **ePublications** section of the gallery on the right.

4. Click to select a page size and format for optimal viewing on the device you wish to target. We chose **Kindle Fire Single Page**.

The page size you select will give you the best setup for optimal viewing on a particular device. However, other page sizes (for example, A4) will still display on ePub devices, they will just be a 'best fit' solution.

WritePlus (accessible within PagePlus) provides a great environment for writing flowing text. This is perfect for publishing eBooks. Alternatively, you can work directly on the PagePlus page within text frames.

To add a text frame:

1. On the **Tools** toolbar, click **Standard Text Frame**.

2. Drag to create a text frame which fills most of the page—you can use the blue margin lines that appear to help you place your frame.

You can now type your book directly into the text frame or use WritePlus.

To use WritePlus:

1. With the text frame still selected, on the context toolbar, click **Edit story in WritePlus**.

2. In the **WritePlus** dialog, type your book (remembering to save your work regularly).

> We recommend sticking to websafe fonts when creating your eBook as websafe fonts are available on most computers and eBook readers. This will ensure your eBook displays exactly how you intended on all reading platforms.
>
> **Websafe fonts include:** Arial, Comic Sans MS, Courier New, Georgia, Tahoma, Times New Roman, Trebuchet MS, and Verdana.

To help us progress with this tutorial together, we have provided a short book entitled *Self-publish Your Own eBook* which can be found in the **Tutorials** assets pack. However, feel free to complete the tutorial using a book you have already written in, or imported into, PagePlus.

To add tutorial assets and text styles:

1. Repeat the initial procedure in this tutorial to open another ePublication document with one blank page.

2. Follow the *Using the tutorial Page Content asset* (p. 88) and *Applying text styles* (p. 92) procedures outlined in the *Text styles* tutorial and then continue with this tutorial.

Next we'll explore one main feature about eBooks—the ability to include cross-referencing hyperlinks!

 Don't forget to save your work!

Adding hyperlinks

Hyperlinks are a great way of directing readers to a website which can provide them with more information on the topics discussed in your book or to connect them directly with any referenced material within your book.

> ⚠ Although you can place hyperlinks in your book, not all eBook readers support them. The hyperlinked text will still display but may not redirect to the hyperlinked content. If you have hyperlinked text within your book, you may wish to create a 'References' chapter at the end of your book which provides hyperlink details. See our References section at the end of the tutorial book.

To add hyperlinks to text:

1. On the **Hintline** toolbar, click ▶ **Next Page** several times to reach the **Conclusion** section.

2. Click to select the text frame and then drag to select 'getting published' in the Conclusion section.

3. On the **Standard** toolbar, click 🌐 **Hyperlink**.

4. In the **Hyperlink Properties** dialog:

- Select **An Internet page**.

- In the **URL address on the Internet** input box, type a web address (e.g. http://www.serif.com).

- Click **OK**.

The text will update to a hyperlink format (underlined and shaded) and will also display a hyperlink button when selected.

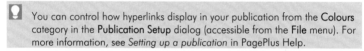

> You can control how hyperlinks display in your publication from the **Colours** category in the **Publication Setup** dialog (accessible from the **File** menu). For more information, see *Setting up a publication* in PagePlus Help.

Before we export our publication as an eBook, we'll quickly design a cover...

Don't forget to save your work!

Designing a cover

You can use any page in your publication as your eBook cover. Currently, all of our page contain text only, which would result in a rather dull cover. So, let's design a cover on a newly created page at the beginning of our publication.

To add a new page:

* On the **Pages** tab, click the first page and then click **Add Page**.

We'll use a background asset to start our design...

To add a background asset:

1. On the **Assets** tab, click Browse to open the **Asset Browser**.

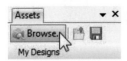

2. In the **Categories** section, click to select the **Backgrounds** category. The backgrounds from all installed packs are displayed in the main pane.

3. In the main pane, the assets are categorized by the Pack file that they belong to. In the **Vector** pack, select a background thumbnail of your choice.

The green 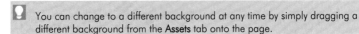 shows that the asset has been added to the tab.

4. Click **Close** to exit.

5. On the **Assets** tab, the **Backgrounds** category should be displayed (if not, click the **Backgrounds** header).

6. Drag the background onto the page.

The background is added to the page as a special background layer and automatically adjusts to fit the page area.

> You can change to a different background at any time by simply dragging a different background from the **Assets** tab onto the page.

Next, we'll add a graphic asset...

To add a graphic asset:

1. On the **Assets** tab, click 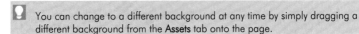 **Browse** to open the **Asset Browser**.

2. In the **Categories** section, click to select the **Graphics** category.

3. In the Search box, type 'butterflies'. All graphics with a "butterflies" tag are listed. Click to select the displayed graphic.

4. Click **Close** to exit.

5. On the **Assets** tab, the **Graphics** category should be displayed (if not, click the **Graphics** header).

6. Drag the graphic onto the page.

7. With the graphic still selected, drag its corner handles to resize it and then position it on the page as desired.

8.   With the graphic still selected, on the **Colours** toolbar, from the **Fill** flyout, select **Scheme Colour 2**.

Finally, let's add the title of our book...

To add artistic text:

1. On the **Tools** toolbar, click the **A** **Artistic Text Tool**.

2. Click anywhere on the page and type 'Self-publish Your Own eBook'. We recommend adding soft returns (**Shift-Return**) after 'publish' and 'Own'.

3.   **A** ˙ Click the border of the artistic text object (it will turn solid), then on the **Colours** toolbar, from the **Text** flyout, select **Scheme Colour 2**.

4. On the context toolbar, set the font and size to **ZapfHumnst Ult BT** and **48 pt**, respectively.

5. On the **Paragraph** tab:

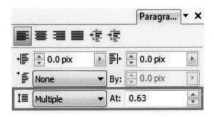

- From the **Line Spacing** drop-down list, select **Multiple**.

- Set the line spacing at **0.63**.

6. Reposition the text object to sit neatly next to the graphic asset.

Your page should now resemble ours...

 We added a logo to the bottom right of our cover to finish it off.

Now we've finished preparing our publication, it's finally time to export it as an eBook!

Don't forget to save your work!

Publishing an eBook

With your book now written, edited, and prepared as discussed above, you are now ready to export it from PagePlus to an eBook format.

To export your publication as an eBook:

- From the **File** menu, select **Publish As>eBook**.

  The **Publish as eBook** dialog will open.

The **Publish as eBook** dialog is so important in getting your eBook right, we're going to step through it carefully...

To set Output settings:

- From the **Profile** drop-down list:

  - Select **Kindle Flowing** if your publication was originally set up for a Kindle device (as we have).

  - Select **Generic Flowing** for all other publication setups.

These presets will ensure your publication is exported using the most appropriate layout and compatibility settings. However, you may wish to update the other Output settings to suit your needs. For more information, see *Publishing as eBooks* in PagePlus Help.

 For **Fixed** layouts and **EPUB 3** compatibility, see the *Creating an image-rich, fixed layout ePublication* tutorial on p. 139.

To set Document Info settings:

1. Select the **Document Info>Metadata** sub-category on the left.

2. In the **Title** input box, type the title of your book (in our case, 'Self-publish Your Own eBook').

3. Fill in the remaining fields (Author, Subject, Publisher, etc,.) as appropriate.

4. In the **ID** field, a **UUID** has already been generated for you—to generate another UUID, click **Generate**.

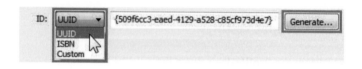

- or -

From the **ID** drop-down list, select **ISBN** and type in your book's ISBN (if required).

- or -

If you have an Amazon ID (ASIN), select **Custom** from the drop-down list and type in your book's ASIN.

The next step will highlight the importance of setting text styles within your publication (see *Applying text styles* on p. 92).

With eBooks, chapters start on a new page.

To set Styles settings:

1. Select the **Styles** sub-category on the left.

2. Click **Heading 1** then:

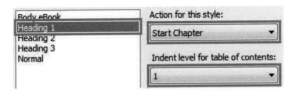

- Set the **Action for this style** as **Start Chapter**.

  This will ensure all Heading 1 style text starts a
  new chapter.

- Set the **Indent level for table of contents** as **1**.

  This will ensure Heading 1 style text appears to the farthest
  left on the table of contents.

3. Click **Heading 2** then:

- Set the **Action for this style** as **Bookmark**.

  This will ensure all Heading 2 style text appears in the table
  of contents.

- Set the **Indent level for table of contents** as **2**.

  This will ensure Heading 2 style text appears indented from
  the chapter titles in the table of contents.

Now to ensure our cover appears correctly in the eBook...

To set cover settings:

1. Select the **Cover** sub-category on the left.

2. Select the **Use Page** option and select the first page in your publication.

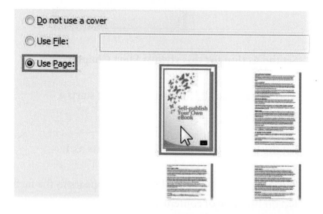

> Alternatively, you can choose to include a bitmap image for your cover using the **Use File** option. Click **Browse**, navigate to your image file and click **Open**. If you do so, you will not need a first page cover design as we have in this tutorial.

If your publication was originally set up for a Kindle device and you still wish your eBook to be viewed on a Kindle device (or Kindle application), you will need to export your eBook as a *.mobi file. Alternatively, you can skip this step and export your eBook directly as an *.epub file for non-Kindle devices and applications.

(Optional) To create a MOBI file for Kindle:

1. Select the **Kindle** category on the left.

2. Click **Download Kindlegen from Amazon** and follow the procedures to download the **Kindlegen.exe** file.

3. Back in PagePlus, click **Browse** and then locate **Kindlegen.exe** and click **Open**.

Now to finish the exporting of your publication to an eBook!

To complete your eBook creation:

1. In the **Publish as eBook** dialog, click **Publish**.

2. In the **Publish eBook** dialog:

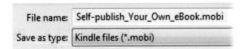

- Navigate to your chosen location.

- Type in a **File name** for your eBook.

- (Optional) From the **Save as type** drop-down list, select **Kindle files (*.mobi)**.

  This option is only available if you followed the *To create a MOBI file for Kindle* procedure above.

- Click **Save**.

If there are any problems with your eBook, in PagePlus the **Preflight** tab will open displaying all the issues. If you added hyperlinks to your publication, these will be highlighted in the tab. The front cover design will also trigger off warnings in the tab.

For more information about the Preflight tab and resolving issues, see *eBook publishing warnings (EPUB 2)* in PagePlus Help.

PagePlus will export your publication as an eBook ready for you to view in your eBook PC reader application.

That's it! You have now created an eBook ready for sharing.

The next stage of the eBook publishing process is to submit your eBook to Amazon and other online stores. Start by visiting the *Kindle Direct Publishing* portal (https://kdp.amazon.com) and reading the guidelines. Other online stores will have similar steps that you can follow.

 There are a variety of devices which allow you to preview your kindle book (*.mobi) on your computer, however, if you install Kindle Previewer software (available from Amazon Kindle publishing), you can also use this as a way to validate the content formatting of your book to ensure it will display correctly on the entire range of Kindle devices and applications.

Creating an image-rich, fixed layout ePublication

 30 min

In this tutorial, we'll walk you through creating an ePublication which is rich in images and publish it in the EPUB 3 format. We'll be using a children's picture book as an example, but the EPUB 3 format is also ideal for other books and publications which are image-rich such as magazines and comics, and text books.

By the end of this tutorial you will be able to:

- Use Page assets to quickly set up a publication.

- Run a manual preflight for your publication to check for problems.

- Export your publication to an EPUB 3 format.

- Modify text wrapping to improve publication export.

Let's begin...

1. From the **File** menu, click **Startup Assistant**.

2. On the left, click **New Publication**.

3. Scroll down to the **ePublications** section of the gallery on the right.

4. Click to select a page size and format for optimal viewing on the device you wish to target. We chose **Kindle Fire Facing Page**.

The page size you select will give you the best setup for optimal viewing on a particular device. However, other page sizes (for example, A4) will still display on ePub devices, they will just be a 'best fit' solution.

To help us progress with this tutorial together, we have provided the beginning of a children's book entitled *Autumn Days* which can be found in the **Tutorials** assets pack.

Setting up our publication

Our short book will ensure we can work through the tutorial and concentrate on the main learning objectives. However, feel free to complete the tutorial using a book you have already written in, or imported into, PagePlus.

To add tutorial assets to the Assets tab:

1. On the **Assets** tab, click **Browse** to open the **Asset Browser**.

2. In the **Pack Files** section, select the **Tutorials** pack.

3. In the **Pages** category, click the **AutumnDays01**,
   AutumnDays03, and **AutumnDays04** page thumbnails.
   (Names appear as tooltips.)

The green 🗸 shows that it has been added to the tab.

4. Click **Close** to exit.

The assets are added to the Page category in the Assets tab.

To add pages to the publication:

1. On the **Assets** tab, the **Page** category should be displayed (if
   not, click the **Page** header).

2. Drag the **AutumnDays01** page asset to the page.

3. On the **Hintline** toolbar, click ▶ **Next Page**.

4. Drag the **AutumnDays03** page asset to the double-page spread.

5. Repeat steps 3 and 4 to add **AutumnDays04** page asset.

The pages/spreads are now in place.

Before we publish our publication, we'll run a preflight which will highlight any areas which might cause a problem during exporting.

We'll look at this next.

 Save now! Click **File>Save As**, type in a new name and click **Save**.

Running publication preflight

A preflight check is always initiated when you export your publication as an ePub (eBook), a PDF, or as HTML. However, you can run a preflight check at any point to fix errors as you go along.

To run a manual preflight check:

1. At the bottom of your workspace (just above the Hintline toolbar), click the **Preflight** tab to expand and display its contents.

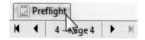

2. On the **Preflight** tab:

- From the **Verify for** drop-down list, select **EPUB 3 Fixed Layout**.

- Click 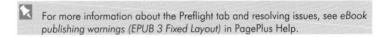 **Check**.

If your publication contains errors, these will be displayed in the tab. Our publication contains the following errors:

- Overflowed text

- Text Frame has wrap shapes

We will look at these errors in turn.

> For more information about the Preflight tab and resolving issues, see *eBook publishing warnings (EPUB 3 Fixed Layout)* in PagePlus Help.

To resolve overflowed text error:

1. On the **Preflight** tab:

- Select the **Overflowed text** error.

- Click  **Locate**.

You will be automatically taken to the object which is causing the error, regardless of which page it is on.

The preflight check has identified the text frame on the right (recto) page of **Page 3** spread.

There is too much content for just a single frame, as indicated by the buttons at the bottom of the frame.

2. Click the [image] **Overflow** button.

The cursor will change to [image] .

3. On the **Hintline** toolbar, click ▶ **Next Page**.

4. Hover over the text frame and click once when the edges glow.

The text flows into the frame, which is now linked to the first frame. Now, let's export this publication as EPUB 3.

 For more information on frame text, see *Frame text* on p. 63 and *Understanding text frames* in PagePlus Help.

 Don't forget to save your work!

Publishing an eBook

With your book now written, edited, and prepared as discussed above, you are now ready to export it from PagePlus to an eBook format.

To export your publication as an eBook:

- From the **File** menu, select **Publish As>eBook**.

  The **Publish as eBook** dialog will open.

The **Publish as eBook** dialog is so important in getting your eBook right, we're going to step through it carefully...

To set Output settings:

- From the **Profile** drop-down list:

  - Select **Kindle Fixed - High Res** if your publication was originally set up for a Kindle device (as we have).

  - Select **iBooks Fixed - High Res** if your publication was originally set up for iBooks.

- Select **Generic Fixed** for all other publication setups.

These presets will ensure your publication is exported using the most appropriate layout and compatibility settings. However, you may wish to update the other Output settings to suit your needs. For more information, see *Publishing as eBooks* in PagePlus Help.

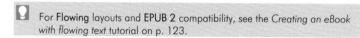

For **Flowing** layouts and **EPUB 2** compatibility, see the *Creating an eBook with flowing text* tutorial on p. 123.

To set Document Info settings:

1. Select the **Document Info>Metadata** sub-category on the left.

2. In the **Title** input box, type the title of your book (in our case, 'Autumn Days').

3. Fill in the remaining fields (Author, Subject, Publisher, etc,.) as appropriate.

4. In the **ID** field, a **UUID** has already been generated for you—to generate another UUID, click **Generate**.

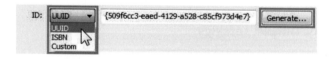

- or -

From the **ID** drop-down list, select **ISBN** and type in your book's ISBN (if required).

- or -

If you have an Amazon ID (ASIN), select **Custom** from the drop-down list and type in your book's ASIN.

> The Styles sub-category allows you to apply actions to the text styles in your publication. For more information on setting text styles and using them in an eBook, see the *Creating an eBook with flowing text* tutorial on p. 123.

Now to ensure our cover appears correctly in the eBook...

To set cover settings:

1. Select the **Cover** sub-category on the left.

2. Select the **Use Page** option and select the first page in your publication.

> Alternatively, you can choose to include a bitmap image for your cover using the **Use File** option. Click **Browse**, navigate to your image file and click **Open**. If you do so, you will not need a first page cover design as we have in this tutorial.

If your publication was originally set up for a Kindle device and you still wish your eBook to be viewed on a Kindle device (or Kindle application), you will need to export your eBook as a *.mobi file. Alternatively, you can skip this step and export your eBook directly as an *.epub file for non-Kindle devices and applications.

To create a MOBI file for Kindle:

1. Select the **Kindle** category on the left.

2. Click **Download Kindlegen from Amazon** and follow the procedures to download the **Kindlegen.exe** file.

3. Back in PagePlus, click **Browse** and then locate **Kindlegen.exe** and click **Open**.

Now to finish the exporting of your publication to an eBook!

To complete your eBook creation:

1. In the **Publish as eBook** dialog, click **Publish**.

2. In the **Publish eBook** dialog:

File name:	Autumn_Days.mobi
Save as type:	Kindle files (*.mobi)

- Navigate to your chosen location.

- Type in a **File name** for your eBook.

- (Optional) From the **Save as type** drop-down list, select **Kindle files (*.mobi)**.

  This option is only available if you followed the *To create a MOBI file for Kindle* procedure on the previous page.

- Click **Save**.

PagePlus will export your publication as an eBook ready for you to view in your eBook PC reader application.

An automatic preflight check will occur on exporting. If you have followed along with this tutorial, you will receive a message confirming the export was successful but that there are still issues with the publication.

If you look at the Preflight tab, you will see the remaining issues involve text wrapping. We'll look at this next.

 Don't forget to save your work!

Updating publication layout

Text wrapped to image outlines is not supported in EPUB 3 format. This issue is present in our publication and highlighted in the Preflight tab. However, PagePlus honours the layout of the publication's pages by converting the text which wraps into images. Although this means your ePublication is replicated precisely, it can result in a higher file size and an inconsistency between the look of page text.

With your eBook PC reader application still open, compare the text on page two and three.

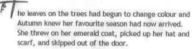

The moral right of the author has been asserted in accordance with the Copyrights, Designs and Patents Act of 1988. All rights reserved.

© Copyright Faye Titaria

No part of this work covered by the copyright thereon may be reproduced or used in any means - graphic, electronic, or mechanical, including copying, recording, taping, or information storage or retrieval systems - without written permission of the publisher.

he leaves on the trees had begun to change colour and Autumn knew her favourite season had now arrived. She threw on her emerald coat, picked up her hat and scarf, and skipped out of the door.

Autumn was so busy wrapping her scarlet and gold scarf around her neck, as she dashed through the woods, she almost tripped over Bertie Hedgehog.

You will notice the text on page two (left) is crisp compared to the text on page three (right). In our PagePlus publication, the text on page two is not wrapped and is exported as text, while the text on page three is wrapped and exported as an image. These issues may not concern you and you may be happy to stick with the current export, but we'll look at how you can update the publication to remove wrapping from text.

To remove text wrapping:

1. On the **Preflight** tab:

    *   Select the **Text Frame has wrap shapes** error.

    *   Click 🔍 **Locate**.

2.   On the context toolbar, click 🖼 **Text Frame Properties**.

3.   In the **Frame Properties** dialog:

•   Select the **General** category on the left.

•   Ensure the **Wrap Text Around Objects** option is deselected.

•   Click **OK**.

The frame text updates so it no longer wraps around the pictures on the page. You will then need to resize the text frame and pictures to ensure they display neatly on the page.

Repeat the above procedure to remove text wrapping from any other text frames listed and then neaten up the page layout.

We used the **Square Crop Tool** to remove the right side of the picture of the branches.

Repeat the *Publishing an eBook* procedure on p. 145 to republish your publication. The eBook settings should be saved to allow you to quickly republish it.

If you saved your updated ePublication under a new name and did not overwrite your original ePublication, you can see the difference in file size of the books. Our small book with text wrapping is 1.9MB whereas without text wrapping it is 1.3MB.

That's it! You have now created an eBook ready for sharing.

The next stage of the eBook publishing process is to submit your eBook to Amazon and other online stores. Start by visiting the *Kindle Direct Publishing* portal (https://kdp.amazon.com) and reading the guidelines. Other online stores will have similar steps that you can follow.

There are a variety of devices which allow you to preview your kindle book (*.mobi) on your computer, however, if you install Kindle Previewer software (available from Amazon Kindle publishing), you can also use this as a way to validate the content formatting of your book to ensure it will display correctly on the entire range of Kindle devices and applications.

Importing and editing PDFs

20 min

A major PagePlus feature is the ability to import PDF publications and then edit them as desired. In this tutorial, we'll explore the ways in which you can effectively import PDFs and then edit them.

By the end of this tutorial you will be able to:

* Import PDF pages:

    * For editability and accurate representation.

    * For ultimate text editing power.

    * To look identical to the original PDF.

* Edit text from imported PDF pages.

* Replace pictures from imported PDFs.

Let's begin...

For our example, we'll use the scenario of creating a four-page events programme based on a PDF produced in a previous year.

To view our tutorial PDF:

1. With Adobe Reader (or any other PDF viewer) open, from the **File** menu, select **Open**.

2. In the dialog, browse to your **Tutorials** folder.

> In a standard installation, the tutorials files can be accessed from the following location:
>
> C:\Program Files\Serif\PagePlus\X8\Tutorials or
> C:\Program Files (x86)\Serif\PagePlus\X8\Tutorials
>
> However, the path may differ if you changed the installation location.

3. Select **pdf_import.pdf** and click **Open**.

Our tutorial PDF file will open in your PDF viewer.

The file contains a cover page, double-page spread events listing, and back page with advertising. We'll show you how you can import each of these sections to get the best from them. Let's open PagePlus and get started.

Importing to 'Tight'

When importing our PDF, we want to keep our front cover page looking pretty much identical to how it currently appears. However, we will want to edit the date. So, let's import the front cover page into PagePlus with this in mind.

To open a PDF for accurate representation and editing:

1. From the **File** menu, click **Startup Assistant**.

2. On the left, click **Open**.

3. From the **Browse My Computer** section, click **PDF files**.

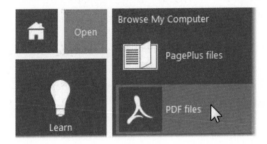

4. In the **Open** dialog, browse to your **Tutorials** folder.

5. Select **pdf_import.pdf** and click **Open**.

All the fonts used in this PDF should be installed on your computer. If you changed the installation settings when installing PagePlus X8, the fonts may not have been installed and you will need to substitute them. For more information, see *Substituting fonts* in PagePlus Help.

6. In the **PDF Import Options** dialog:

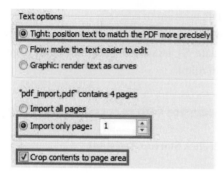

- Select the **Tight...** option.

- Select the **Import only page** option and type **1** in the page input box.

- Ensure the **Crop contents...** option is selected.

    With this option selected, the prepress page marks are removed on import.

- Click **OK**.

PagePlus analyses the PDF and breaks it up into editable sections (such as text frames, images, and shapes). It will match the original design and layout of the PDF as closely as possible.

The **Layers** tab gives an excellent overview of the way PagePlus has broken up the PDF. Now, let's look at the other ways you can import PDFs.

 Save now! Click **File>Save As**, type in a new name and click **Save**.

Importing to 'Flow'

Importing a PDF by flowing the content is very useful if the page contains large sections of text which you wish to edit easily. However, the import may not replicate the page layout as accurately as the other import options.

You can also import PDF pages directly into an open PagePlus publication (as we will do in a moment). This is a great way of collating separate PDFs into a single publication.

To open a PDF for full text editing potential:

1. From the **Insert** menu, select **PDF File**.

2. In the **Open** dialog, browse to your **Tutorials** folder.

3. Select **pdf_import.pdf** and click **Open**.

4. In the **PDF Import Options** dialog:

   - Select the **Flow...** option.

   - Select the **Import only page** option and type **2** in the page input box.

   - Click **OK**.

5. In the **Insert PDF File** dialog:

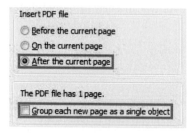

   - Select the **After the current page** option.

   - Ensure the **Group...** option is not selected.

   - Click **OK**.

PagePlus analyses the PDF and breaks it up into editable sections (such as text frames, images, and shapes). It will produce a layout which maximizes the potential for editing text on the page.

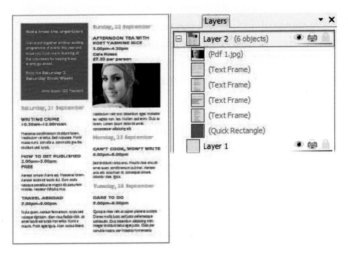

Follow the *To open a PDF for full text editing potential* process again to import the third page of the tutorial PDF.

Now, we'll explore the third import version for PDFs.

 Don't forget to save your work!

Importing to 'Graphic'

The 'Graphic' option for importing PDFs converts all instances of text to shapes and curves. Although this means the text is no longer editable as standard text objects, it does mean the representation of the PDF on the page matches the original PDF with a high degree of accuracy. This is the best option if you do not wish to make any changes to the PDF, or only wish to make changes to colours, shapes, or pictures.

An ideal example of when you might use the graphic import is adding advertising from a sponsor to a publication, if the advert has been designed externally. You can then import the PDF and it will look precisely how the sponsor intended.

Let's work through this scenario by first setting up our page in preparation for receiving our PDF adverts.

To setup your publication page:

1. On the **Hintline** toolbar, click ▶ **Next Page** until the **Page Manager** dialog appears.

2. In the **Page Manager** dialog, accept the default settings and click **OK**.

3. On the context toolbar, click ▦ **Ruler Guides**.

4. In the **Ruler Guides** dialog:

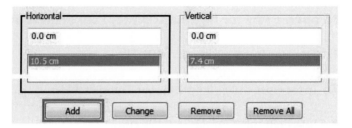

- In the **Horizontal** input box, type **10.5 cm** and then click **Add**.

- In the **Vertical** input box, type **7.4 cm** and then click **Add**.

- Click **OK**.

The page has now been divided up into quarters to allow for the placing of up to four adverts.

> In **Clean Design** mode (default), layout guides only display when an object is created or moved near to them.

To toggle Clean Design view:

- On the **Arrange** toolbar, click ▦ **Clean Design**.

> Still can't see your layout guides? From the **View** menu, ensure that **Guide Lines** and **Bleed Area Guides** are selected from the **Grids and Guides** flyout, and that **Trimmed Mode** is not selected.

> For more information on using guides, see the *Creating page layouts* tutorial on p 19.

Now let's import the first of our adverts.

To open a PDF for highest accuracy representation:

1. From the **Insert** menu, select **PDF File**.

2. In the **Open** dialog, browse to your **Tutorials** folder.

3. Select **pdf_advert01.pdf** and click **Open**.

4. In the **PDF Import Options** dialog:

   - Select the **Graphic...** option.

   - Click **OK**.

5. In the **Insert PDF File** dialog:

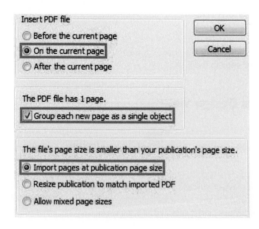

   - Select the **On the current page** option.

- Ensure the **Group...** option is selected.

- Ensure the **Import pages at publication page size** option is selected.

- Click **OK**.

PagePlus imports the PDF as images or shapes. All text in the original PDF is converted to shapes and curves. The other selected options ensure the PDF objects remain grouped for easy organization and that the PDF is placed at its native size on the current page.

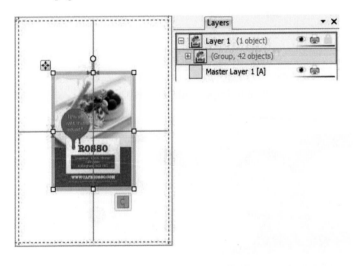

You can reposition the PDF import on your page by dragging the grouped objects. The ruler guides can help you position the advert accurately.

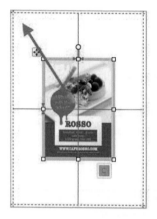

Follow the *To open a PDF for highest accuracy representation* process on p. 162 again to import **pdf_advert02.pdf**.

Depending on the size of the original advert design, you may have to resize the imported objects to fit on your page.

 You may find pressing the **Alt** key as you resize your advert will adjust the design more effectively.

Follow the *To open a PDF for highest accuracy representation* process on p. 162 again to import **pdf_advert03.pdf** and complete the back page design.

 We used the options on the **Arrange** toolbar to change the stacking order of our adverts.

Now all of our PDF pages have been imported into our PagePlus publication, we can look at the different ways they can be edited.

 If you do not intend to modify the PDF in any way, you can place the PDF on the page as a picture. From the **Insert** menu, select **Picture>From File**, and then select **Adobe Acrobat Format (*.pdf)** from the file format drop-down list. For more information, see *Importing PDF files* in PagePlus Help.

 Don't forget to save your work!

Editing text from imported PDFs

The way in which you imported a PDF will determine the ways in which you can edit text on the page.

> For all importing options, pictures and shapes are dealt with in an identical way.

Let's edit some text on a page imported using the **Tight** option. We'll update the dates on the cover.

To edit tight and flow PDF text:

1. Click to select the text frame containing the date.

2. Drag to highlight the dates '21-28'.

3. Type '20-27'.

The text on pages two and three can be edited in an identical way, as these were importing using the **Flow** option.

We also replaced the pictures in the example above. For more information, see the *Replacing pictures from imported PDFs* section on p. 171.

For the graphic PDF import, all text in the original PDF is converted to shapes and curves. Therefore the text on the final page cannot be directly substituted with new text nor have its font changed.

You can edit these objects in other ways, including repositioning, resizing, copying, deleting, and recolouring.

To edit graphic PDF text:

1. Select the bottom advert and click **Ungroup Objects**.

   When ungrouped, you can see each letter and number within the advert has become an individual shape.

2. On the **Tools** toolbar, select the **Pointer Tool**.

3. Position your cursor on the workspace to the top, right of the blue text and drag to draw a marquee around the words.

4. Using the **Colour** or **Swatches** tab, change the fill and line colour of the text shapes.

We used the **Colour Picker** to select the olive green used elsewhere in the advert. For more information, see *Sampling colours* in PagePlus Help.

5. Select the blue line below the price and change the line colour to match the text shapes.

The advert text has now been recoloured.

To keep our work organized, we'll regroup the advert objects.

To group objects:

1. On the **Tools** toolbar, select the **Pointer Tool**.

2. Position your cursor on the workspace to the bottom, right of the page and drag to draw a marquee around the advert.

3. On the object toolbar, click **Group Objects**.

The advert objects are grouped together again for easy management.

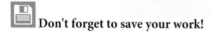 **Don't forget to save your work!**

Replacing pictures from imported PDFs

When PagePlus imports a PDF which contains pictures, each picture is selectable and can be replaced with a picture of your own. If the picture was originally contained in a frame or had some form of effect applied (e.g. a drop shadow), these are imported as separate elements.

You can see this if you look closely at the imported pictures on the first page. They are split into the picture with a separate frame and drop shadow.

Replacing the picture directly is simple...

To quickly replace a picture:

- Drag a picture from the **Pictures** category in the **Assets** tab on top of the picture on the page.

However, we would recommend converting the original picture to a frame before the substitution takes place. This allows you more positioning flexibility once the picture has been replaced.

To replace a picture (recommended):

1. Select a picture.

2. From the **Tools** menu, select **Convert To>Picture Frame**.

3. Drag a picture from the **Pictures** category in the **Assets** tab on top of the picture frame.

4.  Use the picture frame's object toolbar to position the picture within the frame.

You can leave the imported picture elements otherwise unchanged if you like. Alternatively, you can delete the separate frame and drop shadow and reapply these attributes directly to the newly added picture.

That's it! You now know how to work with the different PDF import options available in PagePlus and how to edit text and pictures on your page following import. For more information on working with text and pictures, see the *Working with theme layouts* tutorial on p. 3.

Once you have finished editing your publication, why not export it as a PDF? For more information, see *Publishing PDF files* in PagePlus Help and the *Bleeds and scaling for professional printing* tutorial on p. 35.

 Don't forget to save your work!

Creative
Showcase

2

Pro Templates

PagePlus provides a selection of **Pro Template Pack** publications that are populated with pictures and text placeholders which you can start using straight away.

To open a Pro Template Pack publication:

1. On the **File** menu, click **Startup Assistant**.

2. On the left, click **Templates**.

3. On the **Templates** list, select **Pro Template Packs,** and from the thumbnail gallery, click to select a publication from one of the PagePlus X8 Pro Templates.

4. Click **OK**.

We'll showcase the **Ready Digital Marketing** (as selected above), **Stack & Stone** and **Ski Resort & Leisure** templates next.

 You can get more **Pro Template Packs** from Serif's template store. Visit http://www.serif.com/templates

Ready Digital Marketing

Stack & Stone

Ski Resort & Leisure

Theme Layouts

PagePlus provides **Theme Layout** templates with picture and text placeholders you can use as starting points for your publications.

To open a theme layout publication:

1. On the **File** menu, click **Startup Assistant**.

2. On the left, click **Templates**.

3. On the **Templates** list, select **Theme Layouts**, and from the thumbnail gallery, click to select a publication from one of the Theme Layout templates.

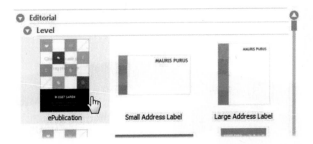

4. (Optional) For multi-page publications, select your pages.

5. Click **OK**.

We'll showcase the **Level** (as selected above), **Partition** and **Geo** templates next.

 For more information, see the *Working with theme layouts* tutorial on p. 3.

Level

Partition

Geo